The Co-Operative Revolution

CO-OP CITY
DEPARTMENT OF PUBLIC SAFETY
POLICE N.Y.
UNITY
CHDA

A Graphic Novel

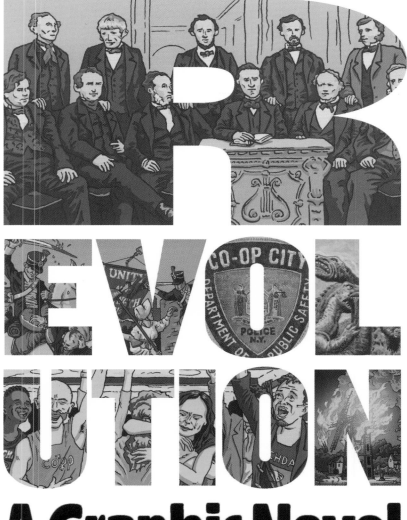

The Co-operative Revolution

First published in 2012 by New Internationalist Publications Ltd on behalf of
The Co-operative Group

New Internationalist Publications
55 Rectory Road
Oxford
OX4 1 BW
UK
newint.org

The Co-operative Group
New Century House
Corporation Street
Manchester
M60 4ES
UK
www.co-operative.coop/graphicnovel

Script and artwork: Polyp

Editors: Paul Monaghan and Claire Ebrey

Contributors: Paul Monaghan, Rachael Vorburg-Rugh, Gillian Lonergan,
Ed Mayo

Front cover: Polyp and Ian Nixon

Design and production: New Internationalist

Mars landing caption: Samuel Wheeler

Printed in the UK on 100% post-consumer recycled paper by Warners, who hold
environmental accreditation ISO 14001.

British Library Cataloguing-in-Publication Data
A catalogue record for this book is available from the British Library.

Library of Congress Cataloging-in-Publication Data
A catalog record for this book is available from the Library of Congress.

ISBN: 978-1-78026-082-2

Contents

Yesterday

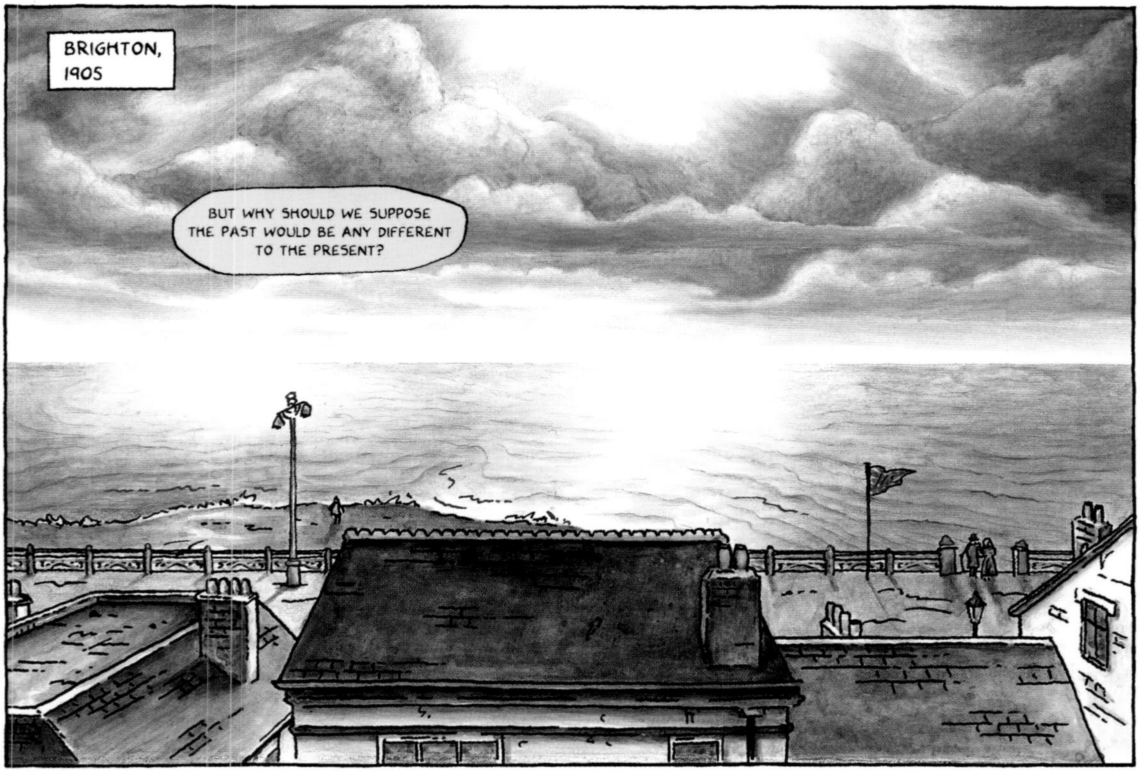
BRIGHTON, 1905
BUT WHY SHOULD WE SUPPOSE THE PAST WOULD BE ANY DIFFERENT TO THE PRESENT?

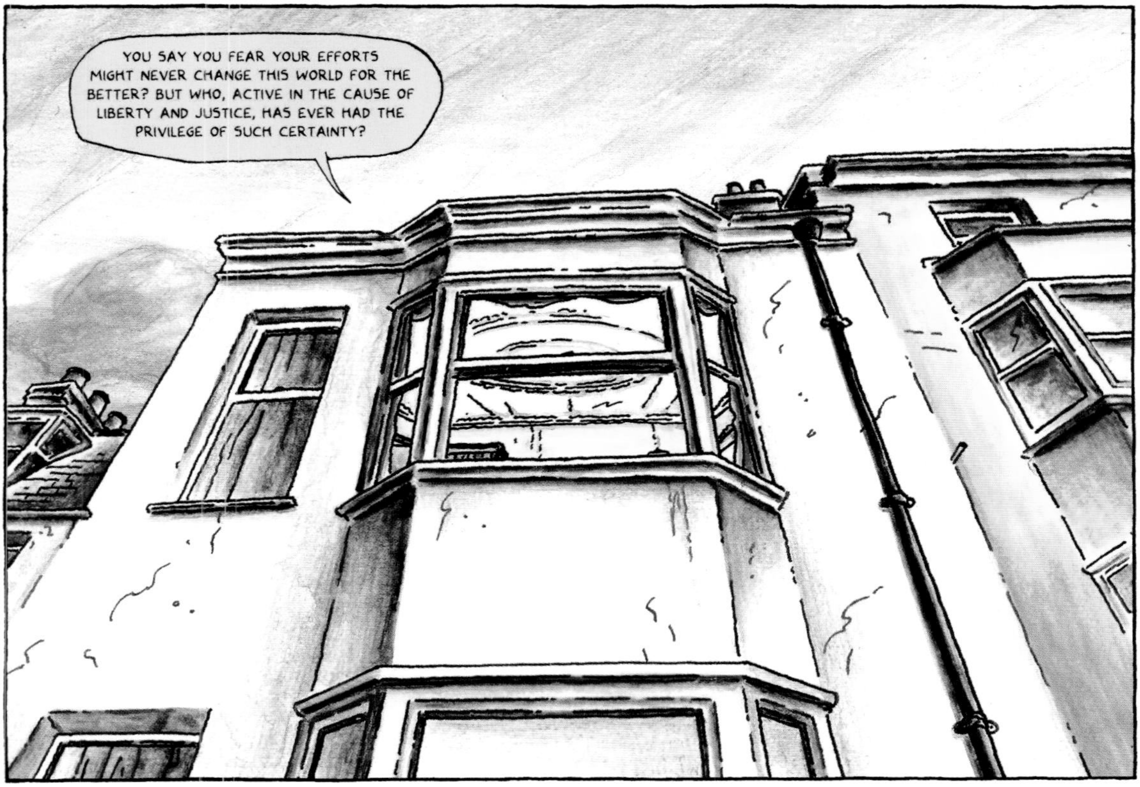
YOU SAY YOU FEAR YOUR EFFORTS MIGHT NEVER CHANGE THIS WORLD FOR THE BETTER? BUT WHO, ACTIVE IN THE CAUSE OF LIBERTY AND JUSTICE, HAS EVER HAD THE PRIVILEGE OF SUCH CERTAINTY?

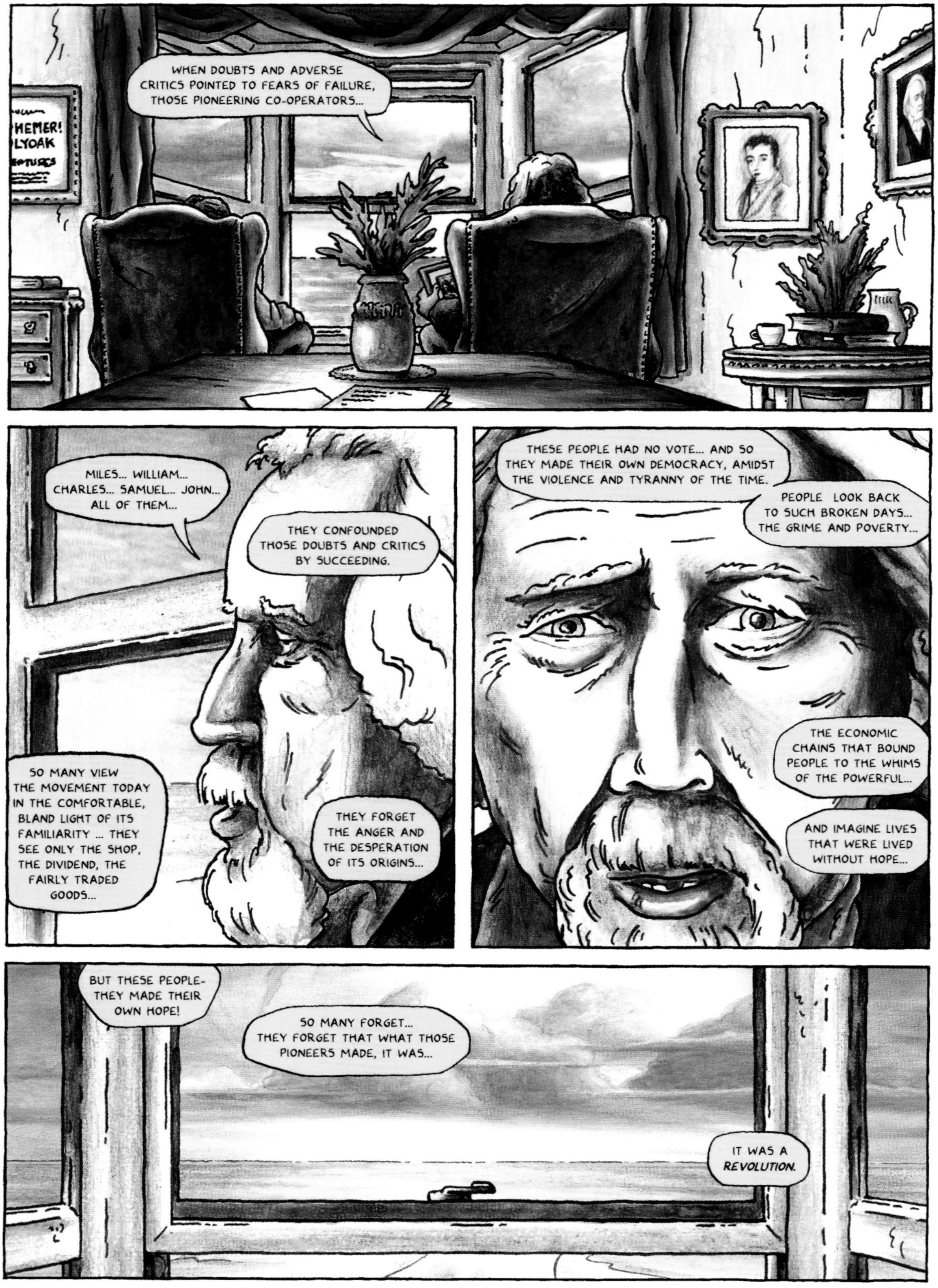
WHEN DOUBTS AND ADVERSE CRITICS POINTED TO FEARS OF FAILURE, THOSE PIONEERING CO-OPERATORS...
MILES... WILLIAM... CHARLES... SAMUEL... JOHN... ALL OF THEM...
THEY CONFOUNDED THOSE DOUBTS AND CRITICS BY SUCCEEDING.
SO MANY VIEW THE MOVEMENT TODAY IN THE COMFORTABLE, BLAND LIGHT OF ITS FAMILIARITY ... THEY SEE ONLY THE SHOP, THE DIVIDEND, THE FAIRLY TRADED GOODS...
THEY FORGET THE ANGER AND THE DESPERATION OF ITS ORIGINS...
THESE PEOPLE HAD NO VOTE... AND SO THEY MADE THEIR OWN DEMOCRACY, AMIDST THE VIOLENCE AND TYRANNY OF THE TIME.
PEOPLE LOOK BACK TO SUCH BROKEN DAYS... THE GRIME AND POVERTY...
THE ECONOMIC CHAINS THAT BOUND PEOPLE TO THE WHIMS OF THE POWERFUL...
AND IMAGINE LIVES THAT WERE LIVED WITHOUT HOPE...
BUT THESE PEOPLE- THEY MADE THEIR OWN HOPE!
SO MANY FORGET... THEY FORGET THAT WHAT THOSE PIONEERS MADE, IT WAS...
IT WAS A *REVOLUTION.*

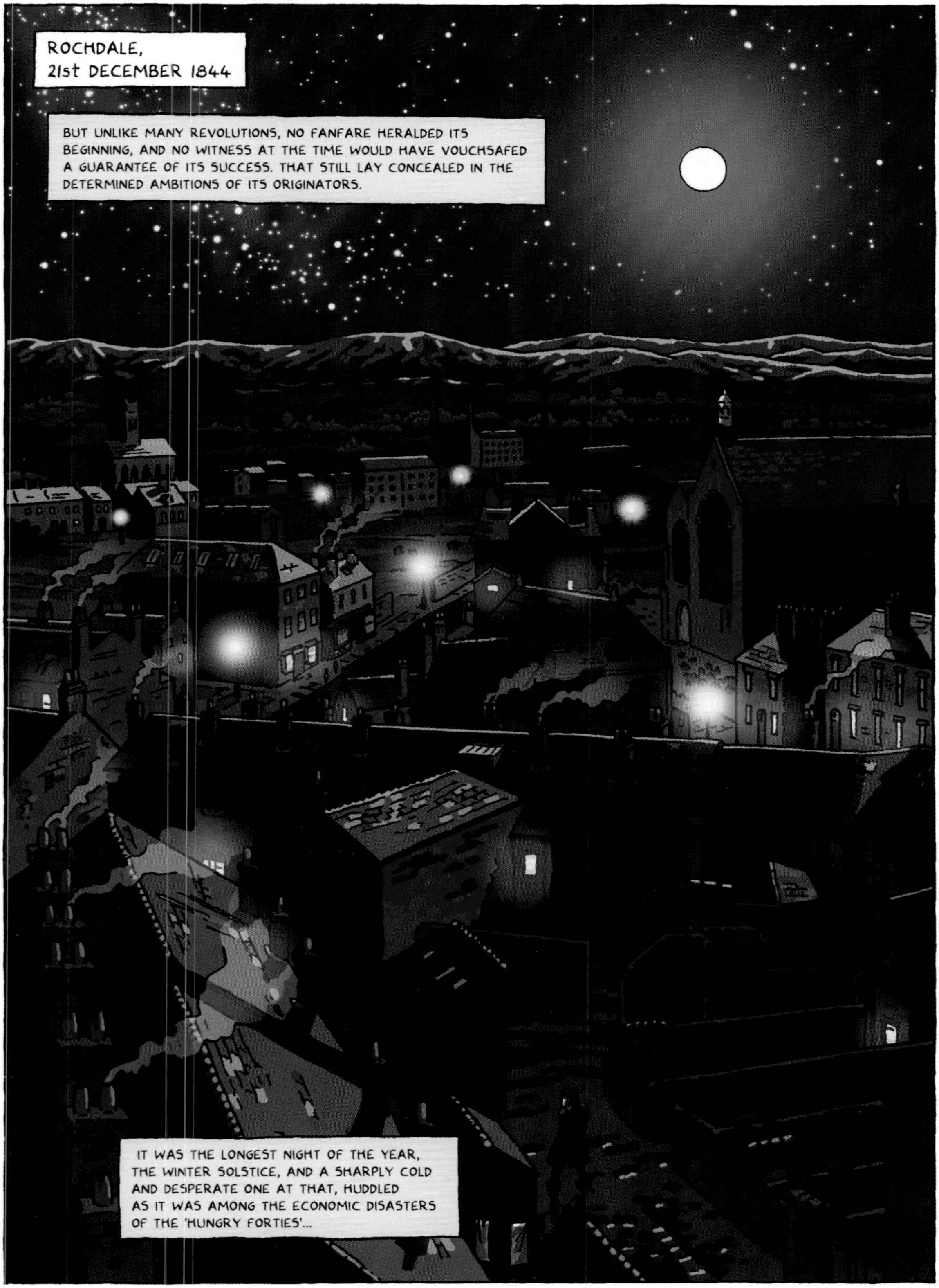
ROCHDALE,
21st DECEMBER 1844
BUT UNLIKE MANY REVOLUTIONS, NO FANFARE HERALDED ITS BEGINNING, AND NO WITNESS AT THE TIME WOULD HAVE VOUCHSAFED A GUARANTEE OF ITS SUCCESS. THAT STILL LAY CONCEALED IN THE DETERMINED AMBITIONS OF ITS ORIGINATORS.
IT WAS THE LONGEST NIGHT OF THE YEAR, THE WINTER SOLSTICE, AND A SHARPLY COLD AND DESPERATE ONE AT THAT, HUDDLED AS IT WAS AMONG THE ECONOMIC DISASTERS OF THE 'HUNGRY FORTIES'...

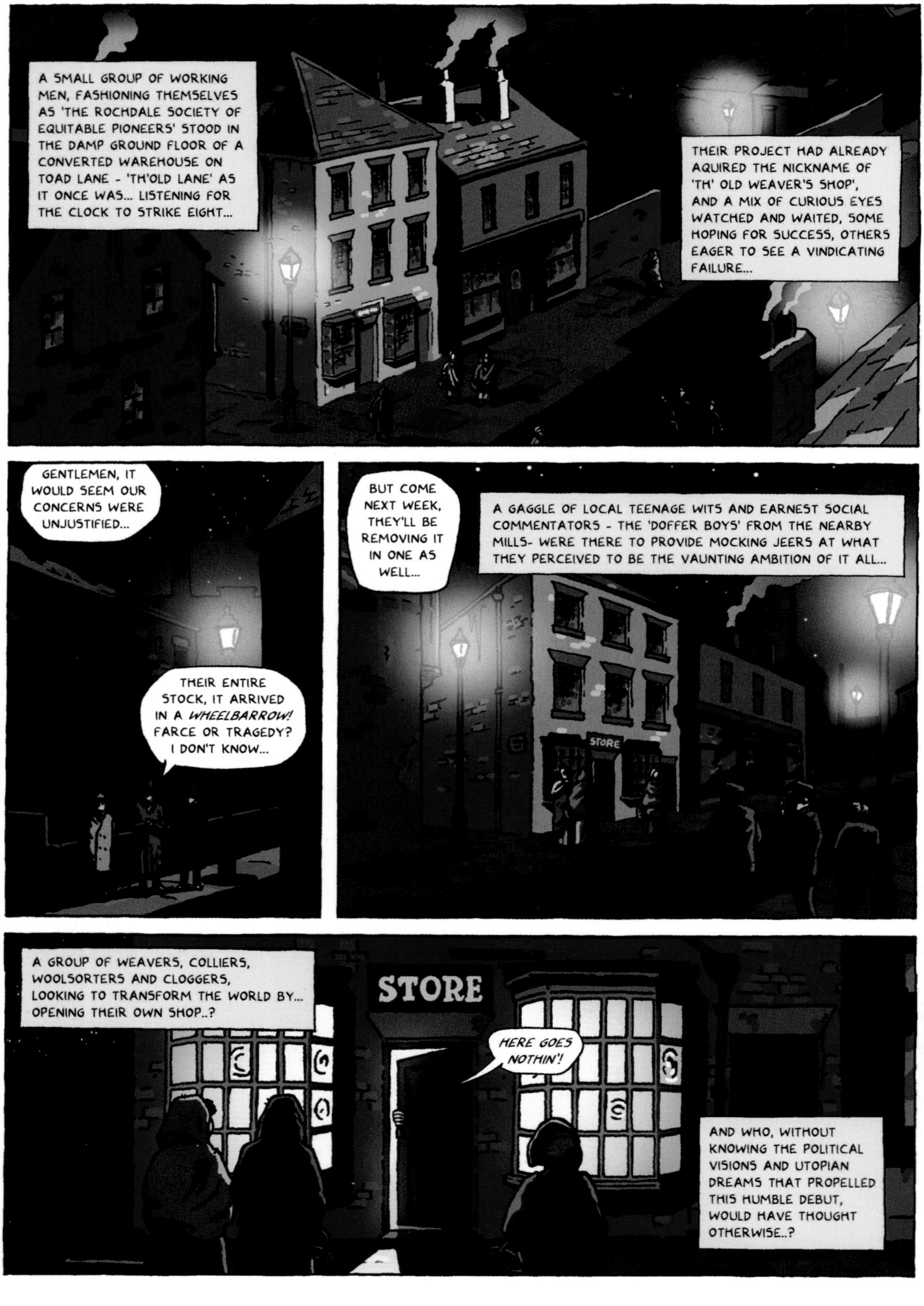
A SMALL GROUP OF WORKING MEN, FASHIONING THEMSELVES AS 'THE ROCHDALE SOCIETY OF EQUITABLE PIONEERS' STOOD IN THE DAMP GROUND FLOOR OF A CONVERTED WAREHOUSE ON TOAD LANE - 'TH'OLD LANE' AS IT ONCE WAS... LISTENING FOR THE CLOCK TO STRIKE EIGHT...
THEIR PROJECT HAD ALREADY AQUIRED THE NICKNAME OF 'TH' OLD WEAVER'S SHOP', AND A MIX OF CURIOUS EYES WATCHED AND WAITED, SOME HOPING FOR SUCCESS, OTHERS EAGER TO SEE A VINDICATING FAILURE...
GENTLEMEN, IT WOULD SEEM OUR CONCERNS WERE UNJUSTIFIED...
THEIR ENTIRE STOCK, IT ARRIVED IN A *WHEELBARROW!* FARCE OR TRAGEDY? I DON'T KNOW...
BUT COME NEXT WEEK, THEY'LL BE REMOVING IT IN ONE AS WELL...
A GAGGLE OF LOCAL TEENAGE WITS AND EARNEST SOCIAL COMMENTATORS - THE 'DOFFER BOYS' FROM THE NEARBY MILLS- WERE THERE TO PROVIDE MOCKING JEERS AT WHAT THEY PERCEIVED TO BE THE VAUNTING AMBITION OF IT ALL...
STORE
A GROUP OF WEAVERS, COLLIERS, WOOLSORTERS AND CLOGGERS, LOOKING TO TRANSFORM THE WORLD BY... OPENING THEIR OWN SHOP..?
STORE
HERE GOES NOTHIN'!
AND WHO, WITHOUT KNOWING THE POLITICAL VISIONS AND UTOPIAN DREAMS THAT PROPELLED THIS HUMBLE DEBUT, WOULD HAVE THOUGHT OTHERWISE..?

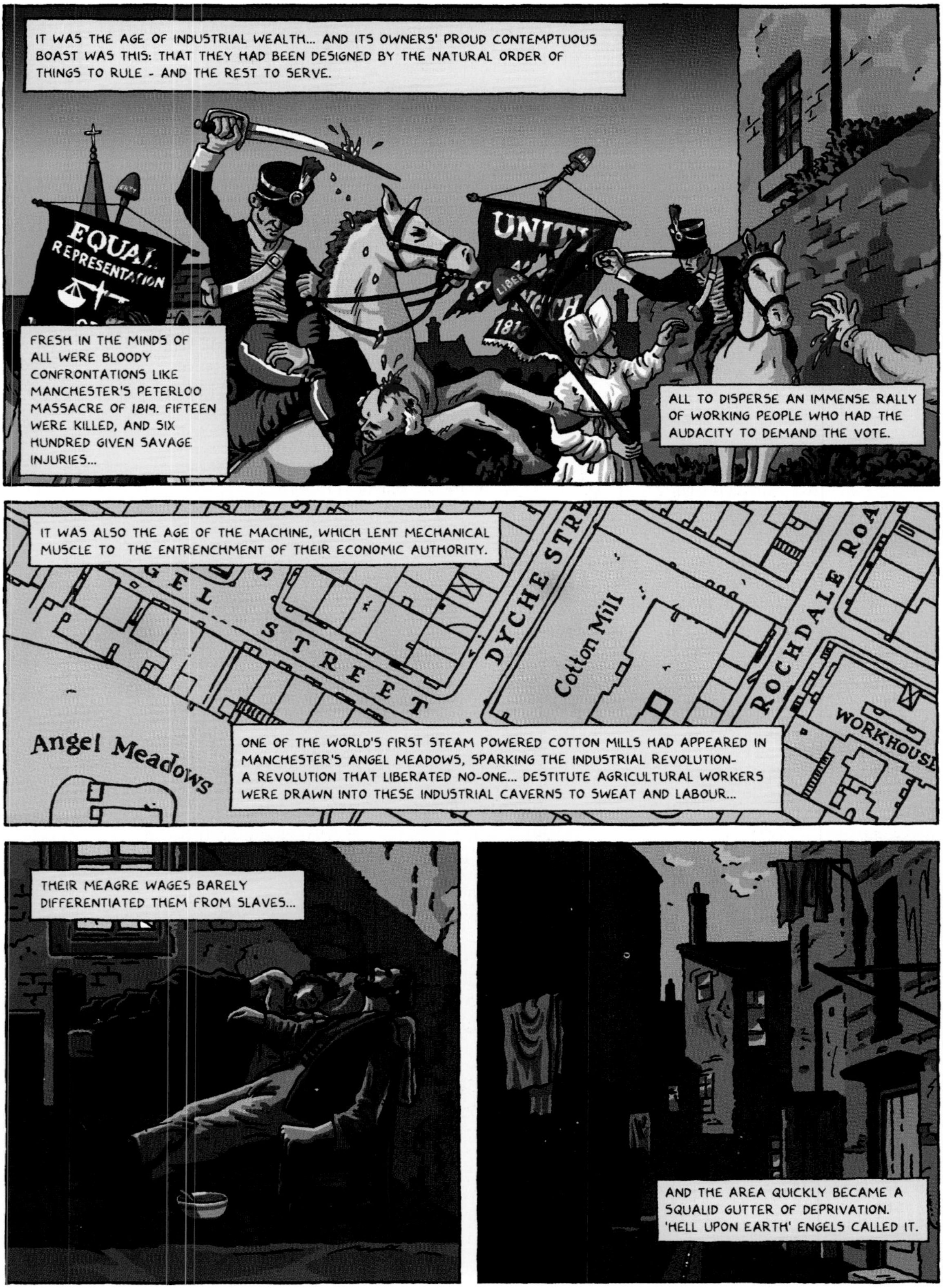
IT WAS THE AGE OF INDUSTRIAL WEALTH... AND ITS OWNERS' PROUD CONTEMPTUOUS BOAST WAS THIS: THAT THEY HAD BEEN DESIGNED BY THE NATURAL ORDER OF THINGS TO RULE - AND THE REST TO SERVE.
EQUAL
REPRESENTATION
UNITY
FRESH IN THE MINDS OF ALL WERE BLOODY CONFRONTATIONS LIKE MANCHESTER'S PETERLOO MASSACRE OF 1819. FIFTEEN WERE KILLED, AND SIX HUNDRED GIVEN SAVAGE INJURIES...
ALL TO DISPERSE AN IMMENSE RALLY OF WORKING PEOPLE WHO HAD THE AUDACITY TO DEMAND THE VOTE.
IT WAS ALSO THE AGE OF THE MACHINE, WHICH LENT MECHANICAL MUSCLE TO THE ENTRENCHMENT OF THEIR ECONOMIC AUTHORITY.
STREET
DYCHE STRE
Cotton Mill
ROCHDALE ROA
WORKHOUSE
Angel Meadows
ONE OF THE WORLD'S FIRST STEAM POWERED COTTON MILLS HAD APPEARED IN MANCHESTER'S ANGEL MEADOWS, SPARKING THE INDUSTRIAL REVOLUTION- A REVOLUTION THAT LIBERATED NO-ONE... DESTITUTE AGRICULTURAL WORKERS WERE DRAWN INTO THESE INDUSTRIAL CAVERNS TO SWEAT AND LABOUR...
THEIR MEAGRE WAGES BARELY DIFFERENTIATED THEM FROM SLAVES...
AND THE AREA QUICKLY BECAME A SQUALID GUTTER OF DEPRIVATION. 'HELL UPON EARTH' ENGELS CALLED IT.

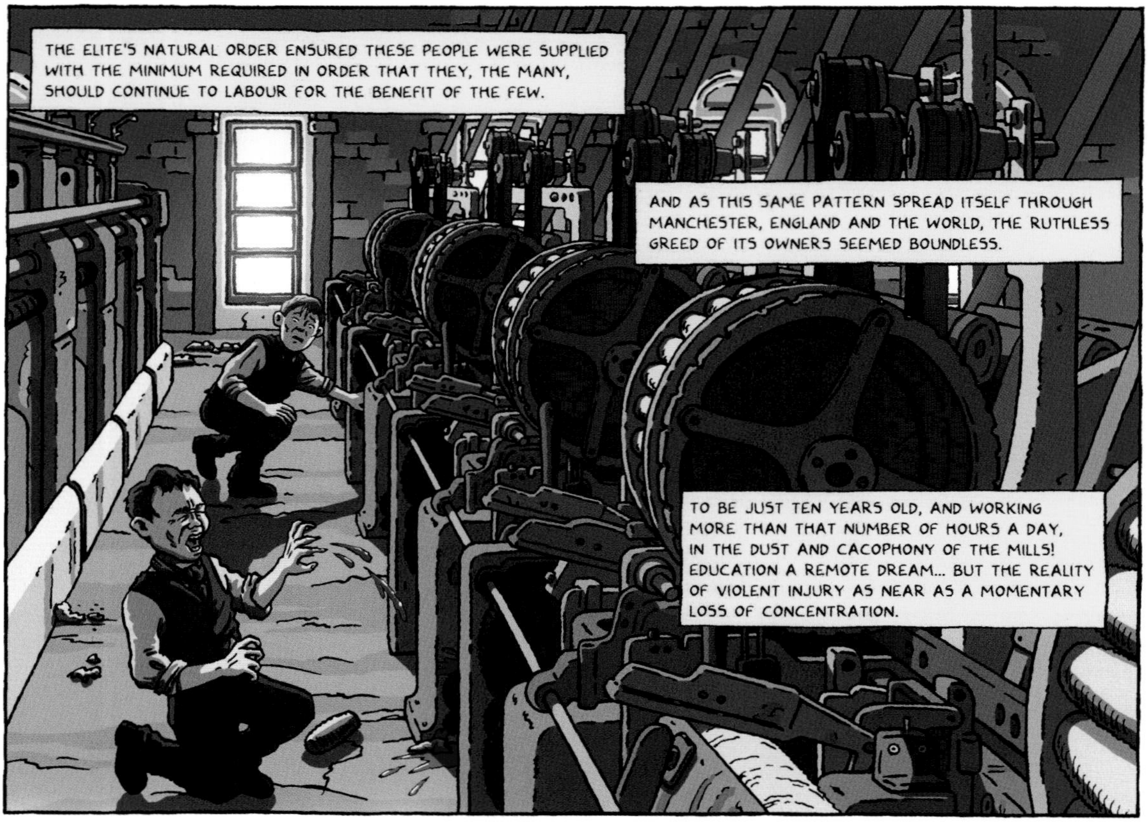
THE ELITE'S NATURAL ORDER ENSURED THESE PEOPLE WERE SUPPLIED WITH THE MINIMUM REQUIRED IN ORDER THAT THEY, THE MANY, SHOULD CONTINUE TO LABOUR FOR THE BENEFIT OF THE FEW.
AND AS THIS SAME PATTERN SPREAD ITSELF THROUGH MANCHESTER, ENGLAND AND THE WORLD, THE RUTHLESS GREED OF ITS OWNERS SEEMED BOUNDLESS.
TO BE JUST TEN YEARS OLD, AND WORKING MORE THAN THAT NUMBER OF HOURS A DAY, IN THE DUST AND CACOPHONY OF THE MILLS! EDUCATION A REMOTE DREAM... BUT THE REALITY OF VIOLENT INJURY AS NEAR AS A MOMENTARY LOSS OF CONCENTRATION.

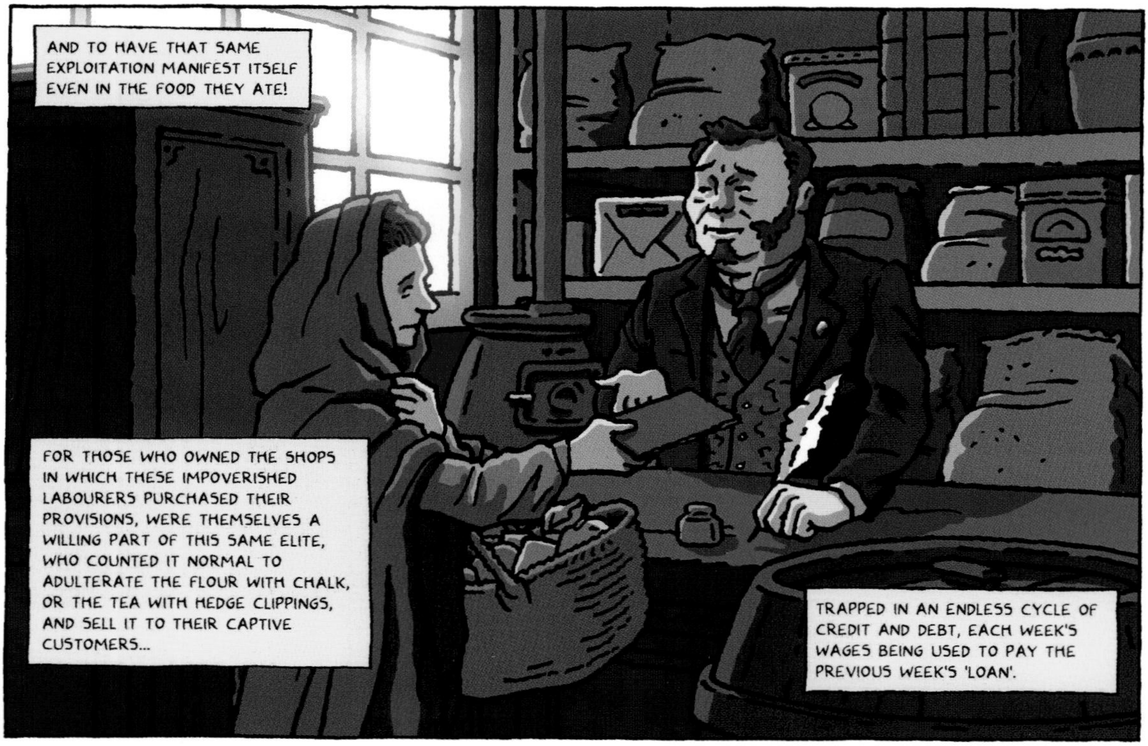
AND TO HAVE THAT SAME EXPLOITATION MANIFEST ITSELF EVEN IN THE FOOD THEY ATE!
FOR THOSE WHO OWNED THE SHOPS IN WHICH THESE IMPOVERISHED LABOURERS PURCHASED THEIR PROVISIONS, WERE THEMSELVES A WILLING PART OF THIS SAME ELITE, WHO COUNTED IT NORMAL TO ADULTERATE THE FLOUR WITH CHALK, OR THE TEA WITH HEDGE CLIPPINGS, AND SELL IT TO THEIR CAPTIVE CUSTOMERS...
TRAPPED IN AN ENDLESS CYCLE OF CREDIT AND DEBT, EACH WEEK'S WAGES BEING USED TO PAY THE PREVIOUS WEEK'S 'LOAN'.

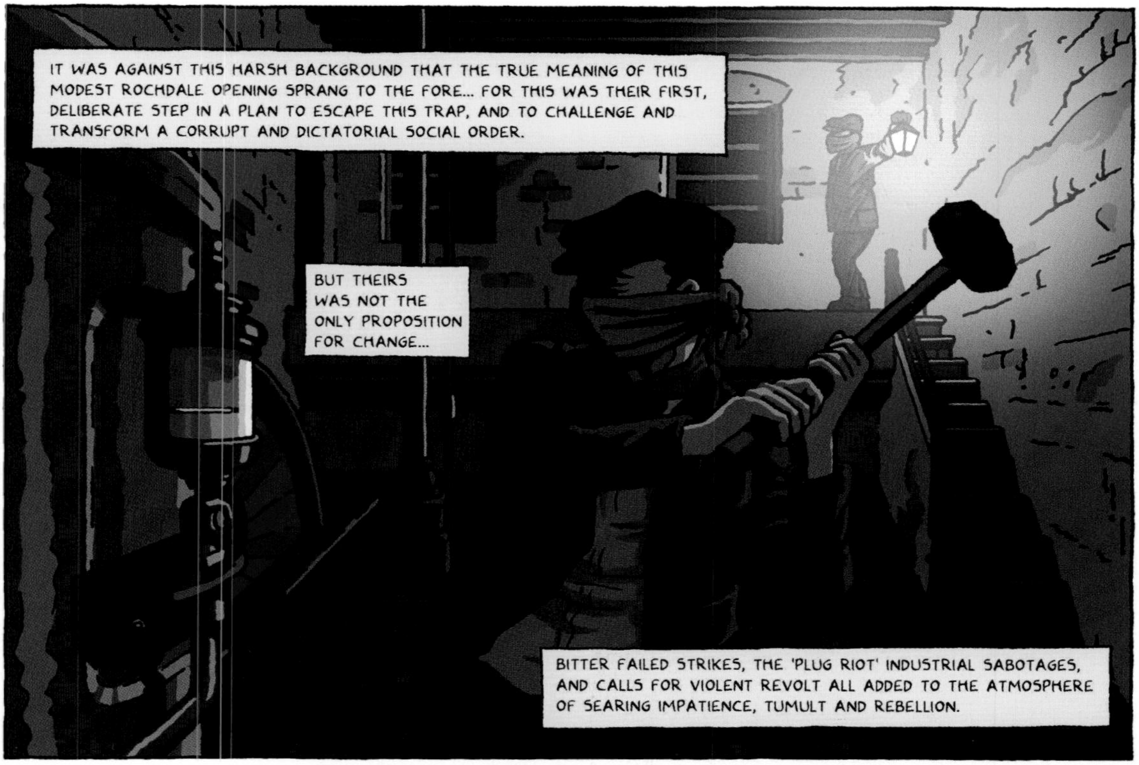
IT WAS AGAINST THIS HARSH BACKGROUND THAT THE TRUE MEANING OF THIS MODEST ROCHDALE OPENING SPRANG TO THE FORE... FOR THIS WAS THEIR FIRST, DELIBERATE STEP IN A PLAN TO ESCAPE THIS TRAP, AND TO CHALLENGE AND TRANSFORM A CORRUPT AND DICTATORIAL SOCIAL ORDER.
BUT THEIRS WAS NOT THE ONLY PROPOSITION FOR CHANGE...
BITTER FAILED STRIKES, THE 'PLUG RIOT' INDUSTRIAL SABOTAGES, AND CALLS FOR VIOLENT REVOLT ALL ADDED TO THE ATMOSPHERE OF SEARING IMPATIENCE, TUMULT AND REBELLION.

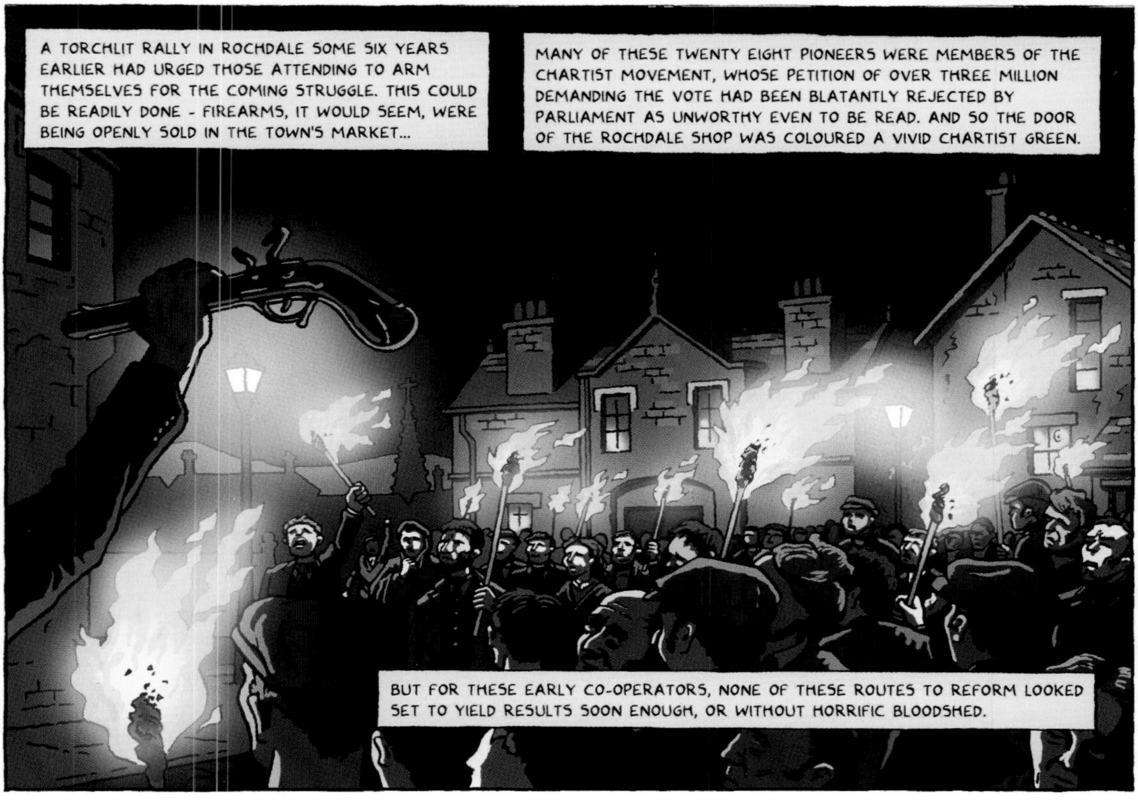
A TORCHLIT RALLY IN ROCHDALE SOME SIX YEARS EARLIER HAD URGED THOSE ATTENDING TO ARM THEMSELVES FOR THE COMING STRUGGLE. THIS COULD BE READILY DONE - FIREARMS, IT WOULD SEEM, WERE BEING OPENLY SOLD IN THE TOWN'S MARKET...
MANY OF THESE TWENTY EIGHT PIONEERS WERE MEMBERS OF THE CHARTIST MOVEMENT, WHOSE PETITION OF OVER THREE MILLION DEMANDING THE VOTE HAD BEEN BLATANTLY REJECTED BY PARLIAMENT AS UNWORTHY EVEN TO BE READ. AND SO THE DOOR OF THE ROCHDALE SHOP WAS COLOURED A VIVID CHARTIST GREEN.
BUT FOR THESE EARLY CO-OPERATORS, NONE OF THESE ROUTES TO REFORM LOOKED SET TO YIELD RESULTS SOON ENOUGH, OR WITHOUT HORRIFIC BLOODSHED.

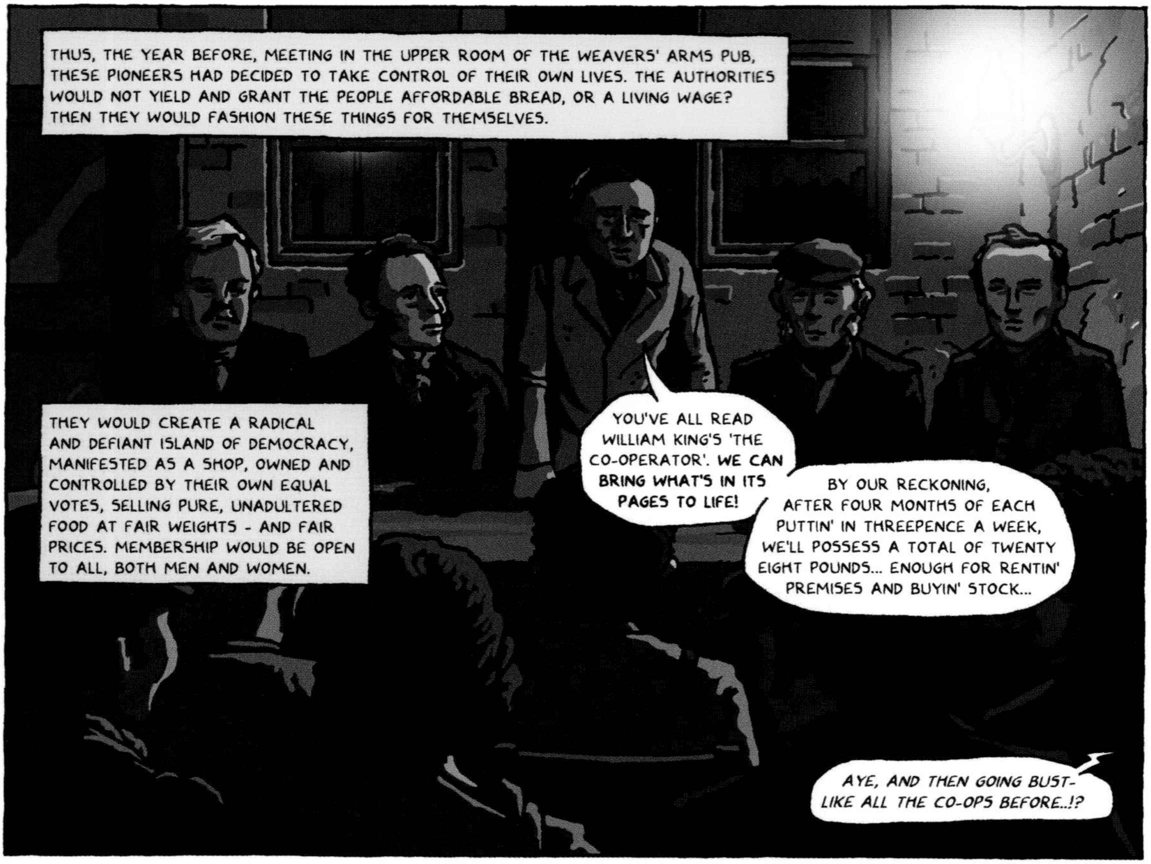
THUS, THE YEAR BEFORE, MEETING IN THE UPPER ROOM OF THE WEAVERS' ARMS PUB, THESE PIONEERS HAD DECIDED TO TAKE CONTROL OF THEIR OWN LIVES. THE AUTHORITIES WOULD NOT YIELD AND GRANT THE PEOPLE AFFORDABLE BREAD, OR A LIVING WAGE? THEN THEY WOULD FASHION THESE THINGS FOR THEMSELVES.
THEY WOULD CREATE A RADICAL AND DEFIANT ISLAND OF DEMOCRACY, MANIFESTED AS A SHOP, OWNED AND CONTROLLED BY THEIR OWN EQUAL VOTES, SELLING PURE, UNADULTERED FOOD AT FAIR WEIGHTS - AND FAIR PRICES. MEMBERSHIP WOULD BE OPEN TO ALL, BOTH MEN AND WOMEN.
YOU'VE ALL READ WILLIAM KING'S 'THE CO-OPERATOR'. **WE CAN BRING WHAT'S IN ITS PAGES TO LIFE!**
BY OUR RECKONING, AFTER FOUR MONTHS OF EACH PUTTIN' IN THREEPENCE A WEEK, WE'LL POSSESS A TOTAL OF TWENTY EIGHT POUNDS... ENOUGH FOR RENTIN' PREMISES AND BUYIN' STOCK...
AYE, AND THEN GOING BUST- LIKE ALL THE CO-OPS BEFORE..!?

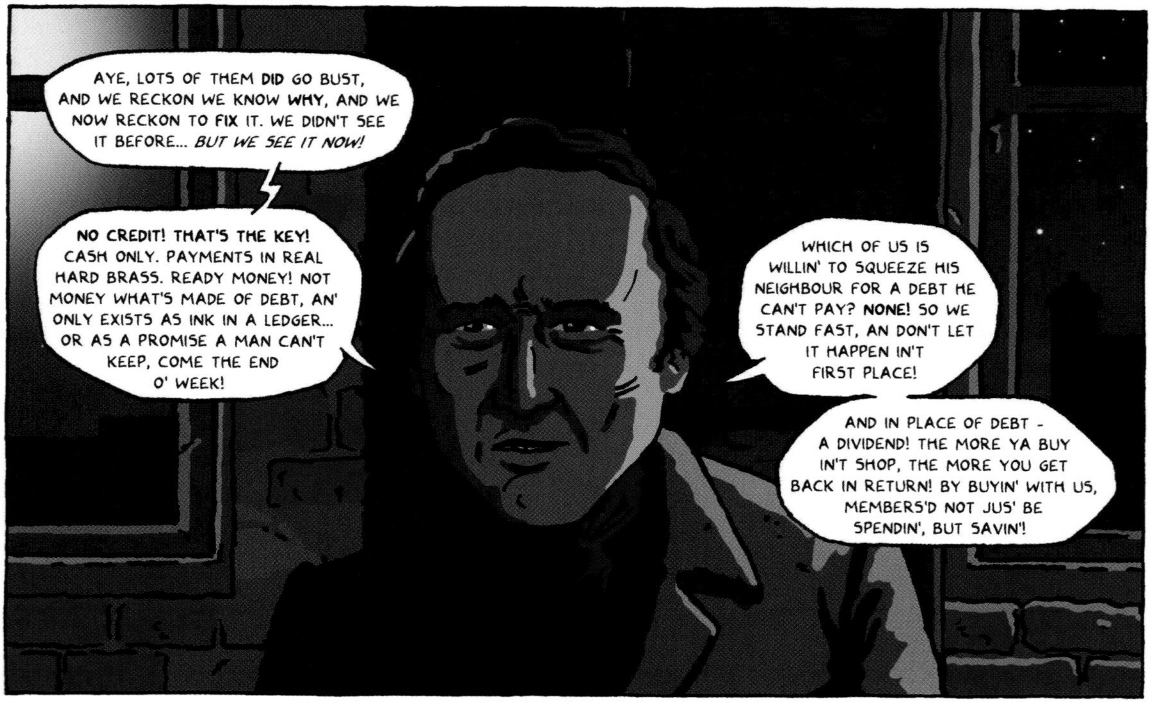
AYE, LOTS OF THEM **DID** GO BUST, AND WE RECKON WE KNOW **WHY**, AND WE NOW RECKON TO **FIX** IT. WE DIDN'T SEE IT BEFORE... *BUT WE SEE IT NOW!*
NO CREDIT! THAT'S THE KEY! CASH ONLY. PAYMENTS IN REAL HARD BRASS. READY MONEY! NOT MONEY WHAT'S MADE OF DEBT, AN' ONLY EXISTS AS INK IN A LEDGER... OR AS A PROMISE A MAN CAN'T KEEP, COME THE END O' WEEK!
WHICH OF US IS WILLIN' TO SQUEEZE HIS NEIGHBOUR FOR A DEBT HE CAN'T PAY? **NONE!** SO WE STAND FAST, AN DON'T LET IT HAPPEN IN'T FIRST PLACE!
AND IN PLACE OF DEBT - A DIVIDEND! THE MORE YA BUY IN'T SHOP, THE MORE YOU GET BACK IN RETURN! BY BUYIN' WITH US, MEMBERS'D NOT JUS' BE SPENDIN', BUT SAVIN'!

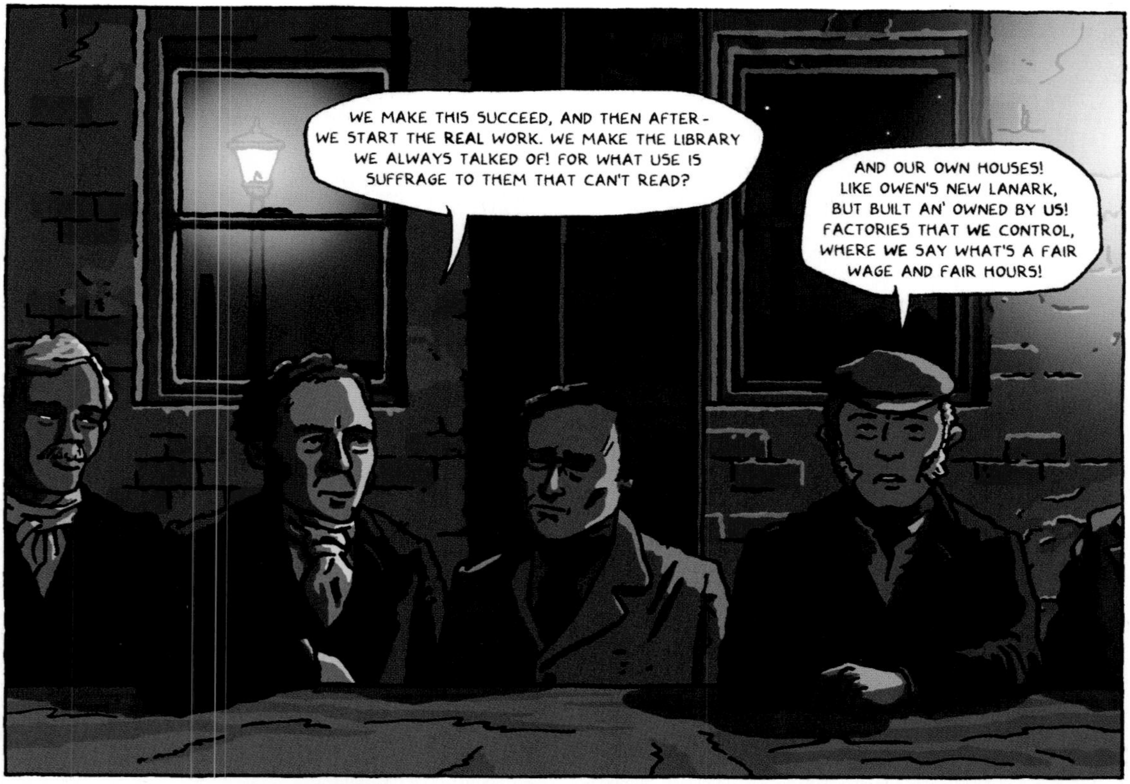
WE MAKE THIS SUCCEED, AND THEN AFTER - WE START THE REAL WORK. WE MAKE THE LIBRARY WE ALWAYS TALKED OF! FOR WHAT USE IS SUFFRAGE TO THEM THAT CAN'T READ?
AND OUR OWN HOUSES! LIKE OWEN'S NEW LANARK, BUT BUILT AN' OWNED BY US! FACTORIES THAT WE CONTROL, WHERE WE SAY WHAT'S A FAIR WAGE AND FAIR HOURS!

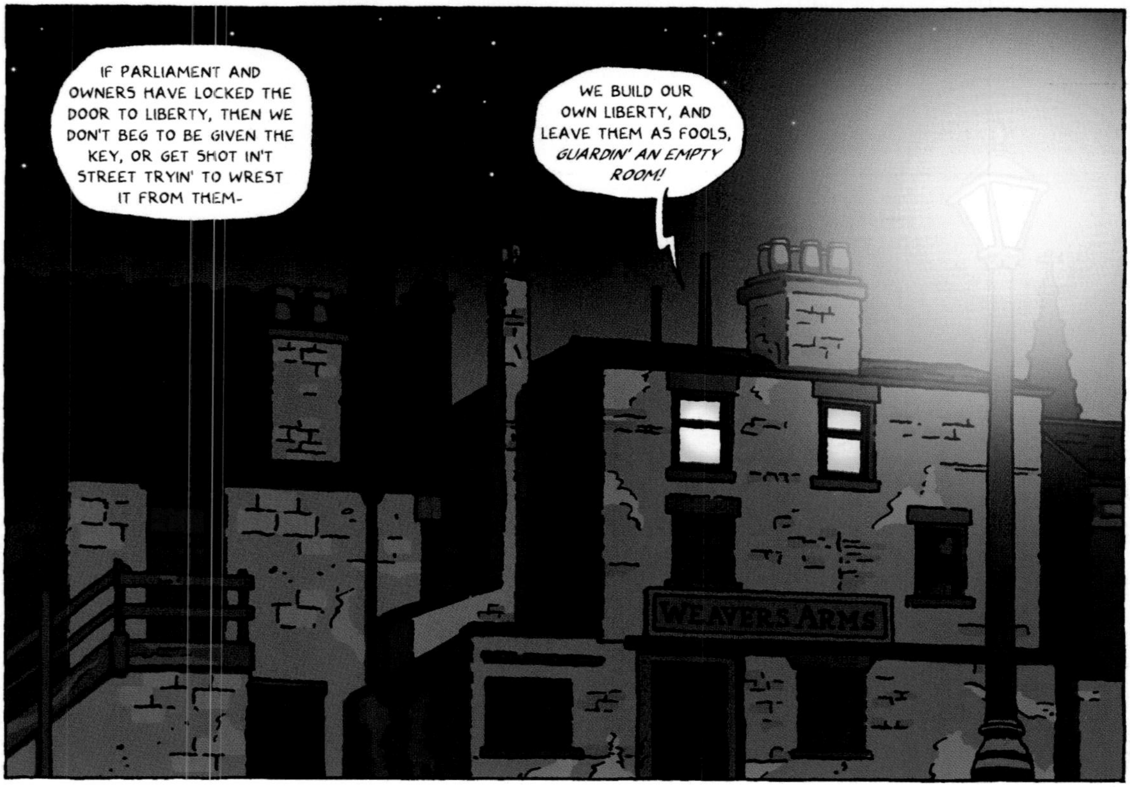
IF PARLIAMENT AND OWNERS HAVE LOCKED THE DOOR TO LIBERTY, THEN WE DON'T BEG TO BE GIVEN THE KEY, OR GET SHOT IN'T STREET TRYIN' TO WREST IT FROM THEM-
WE BUILD OUR OWN LIBERTY, AND LEAVE THEM AS FOOLS, GUARDIN' AN EMPTY ROOM!
WEAVERS ARMS

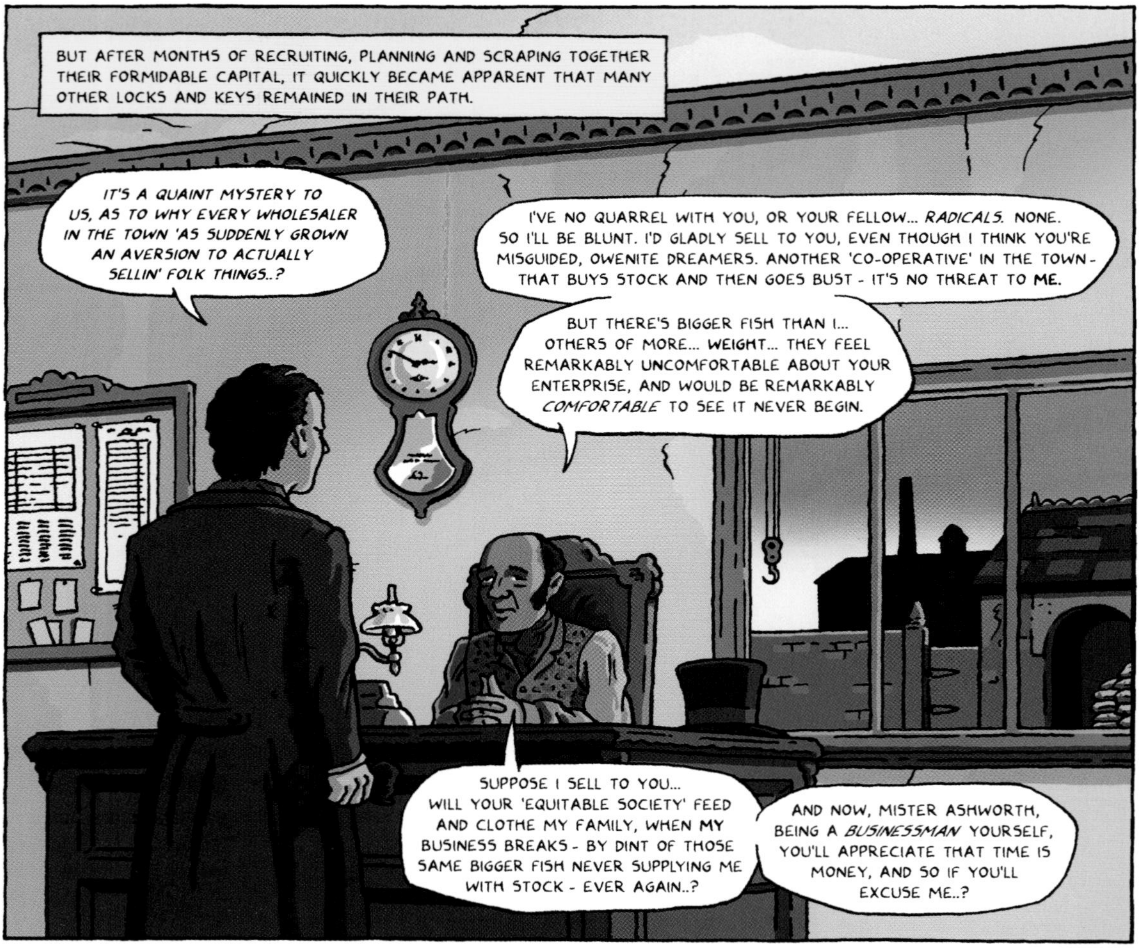
BUT AFTER MONTHS OF RECRUITING, PLANNING AND SCRAPING TOGETHER THEIR FORMIDABLE CAPITAL, IT QUICKLY BECAME APPARENT THAT MANY OTHER LOCKS AND KEYS REMAINED IN THEIR PATH.
IT'S A QUAINT MYSTERY TO US, AS TO WHY EVERY WHOLESALER IN THE TOWN 'AS SUDDENLY GROWN AN AVERSION TO ACTUALLY SELLIN' FOLK THINGS..?
I'VE NO QUARREL WITH YOU, OR YOUR FELLOW... RADICALS. NONE. SO I'LL BE BLUNT. I'D GLADLY SELL TO YOU, EVEN THOUGH I THINK YOU'RE MISGUIDED, OWENITE DREAMERS. ANOTHER 'CO-OPERATIVE' IN THE TOWN - THAT BUYS STOCK AND THEN GOES BUST - IT'S NO THREAT TO ME.
BUT THERE'S BIGGER FISH THAN I... OTHERS OF MORE... WEIGHT... THEY FEEL REMARKABLY UNCOMFORTABLE ABOUT YOUR ENTERPRISE, AND WOULD BE REMARKABLY COMFORTABLE TO SEE IT NEVER BEGIN.
SUPPOSE I SELL TO YOU... WILL YOUR 'EQUITABLE SOCIETY' FEED AND CLOTHE MY FAMILY, WHEN MY BUSINESS BREAKS - BY DINT OF THOSE SAME BIGGER FISH NEVER SUPPLYING ME WITH STOCK - EVER AGAIN..?
AND NOW, MISTER ASHWORTH, BEING A BUSINESSMAN YOURSELF, YOU'LL APPRECIATE THAT TIME IS MONEY, AND SO IF YOU'LL EXCUSE ME..?

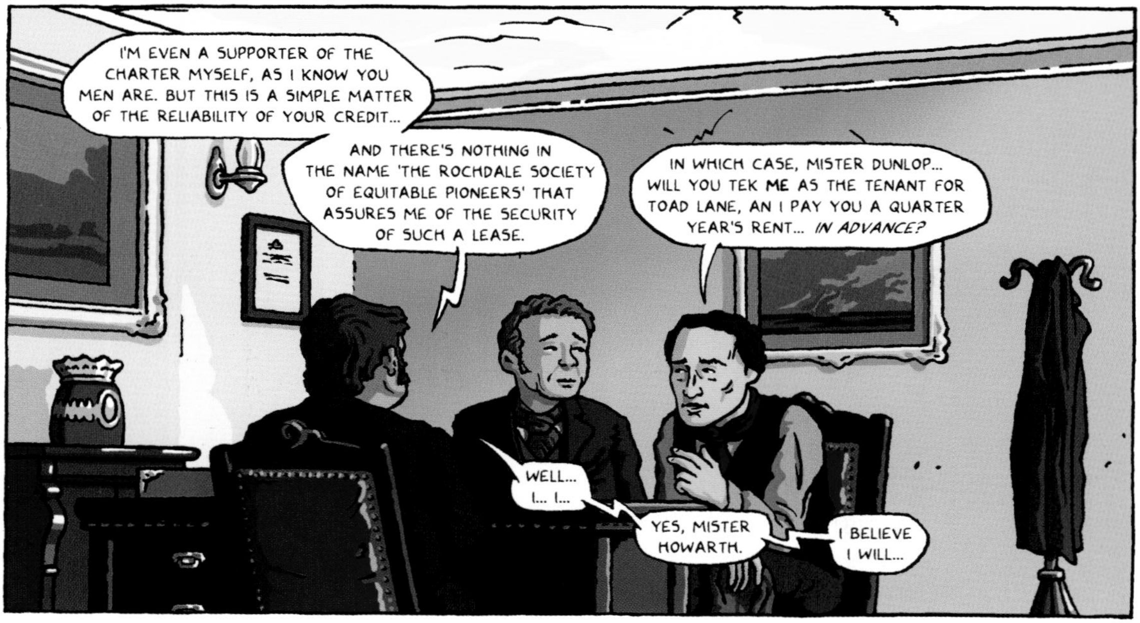
I'M EVEN A SUPPORTER OF THE CHARTER MYSELF, AS I KNOW YOU MEN ARE. BUT THIS IS A SIMPLE MATTER OF THE RELIABILITY OF YOUR CREDIT...
AND THERE'S NOTHING IN THE NAME 'THE ROCHDALE SOCIETY OF EQUITABLE PIONEERS' THAT ASSURES ME OF THE SECURITY OF SUCH A LEASE.
IN WHICH CASE, MISTER DUNLOP... WILL YOU TEK ME AS THE TENANT FOR TOAD LANE, AN I PAY YOU A QUARTER YEAR'S RENT... IN ADVANCE?
WELL... I... I...
YES, MISTER HOWARTH.
I BELIEVE I WILL...

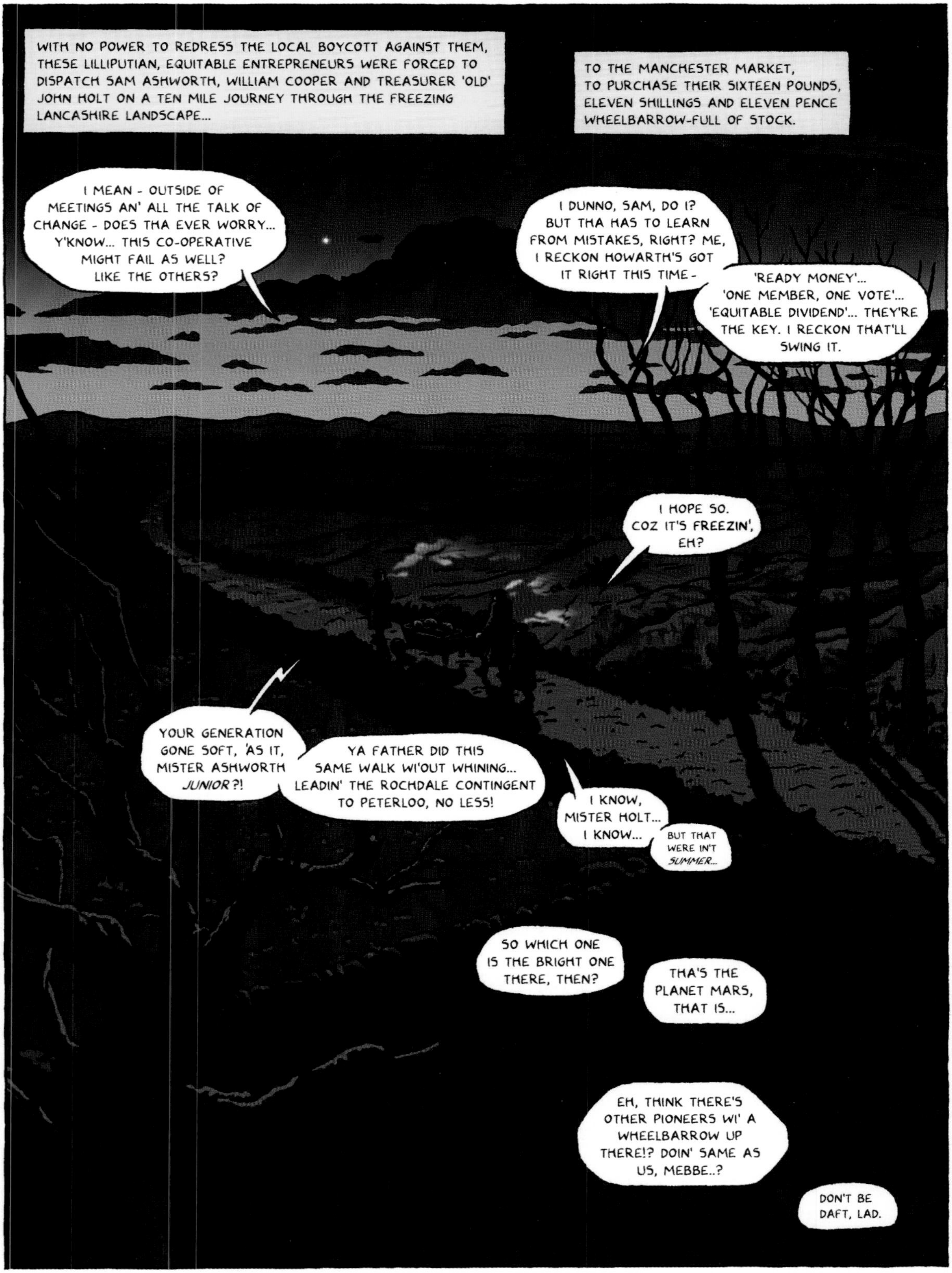
WITH NO POWER TO REDRESS THE LOCAL BOYCOTT AGAINST THEM, THESE LILLIPUTIAN, EQUITABLE ENTREPRENEURS WERE FORCED TO DISPATCH SAM ASHWORTH, WILLIAM COOPER AND TREASURER 'OLD' JOHN HOLT ON A TEN MILE JOURNEY THROUGH THE FREEZING LANCASHIRE LANDSCAPE...
TO THE MANCHESTER MARKET, TO PURCHASE THEIR SIXTEEN POUNDS, ELEVEN SHILLINGS AND ELEVEN PENCE WHEELBARROW-FULL OF STOCK.
I MEAN - OUTSIDE OF MEETINGS AN' ALL THE TALK OF CHANGE - DOES THA EVER WORRY... Y'KNOW... THIS CO-OPERATIVE MIGHT FAIL AS WELL? LIKE THE OTHERS?
I DUNNO, SAM, DO I? BUT THA HAS TO LEARN FROM MISTAKES, RIGHT? ME, I RECKON HOWARTH'S GOT IT RIGHT THIS TIME-
'READY MONEY'... 'ONE MEMBER, ONE VOTE'... 'EQUITABLE DIVIDEND'... THEY'RE THE KEY. I RECKON THAT'LL SWING IT.
I HOPE SO. COZ IT'S FREEZIN', EH?
YOUR GENERATION GONE SOFT, 'AS IT, MISTER ASHWORTH *JUNIOR*?!
YA FATHER DID THIS SAME WALK WI'OUT WHINING... LEADIN' THE ROCHDALE CONTINGENT TO PETERLOO, NO LESS!
I KNOW, MISTER HOLT... I KNOW...
BUT THAT WERE IN'T *SUMMER*...
SO WHICH ONE IS THE BRIGHT ONE THERE, THEN?
THA'S THE PLANET MARS, THAT IS...
EH, THINK THERE'S OTHER PIONEERS WI' A WHEELBARROW UP THERE!? DOIN' SAME AS US, MEBBE..?
DON'T BE DAFT, LAD.

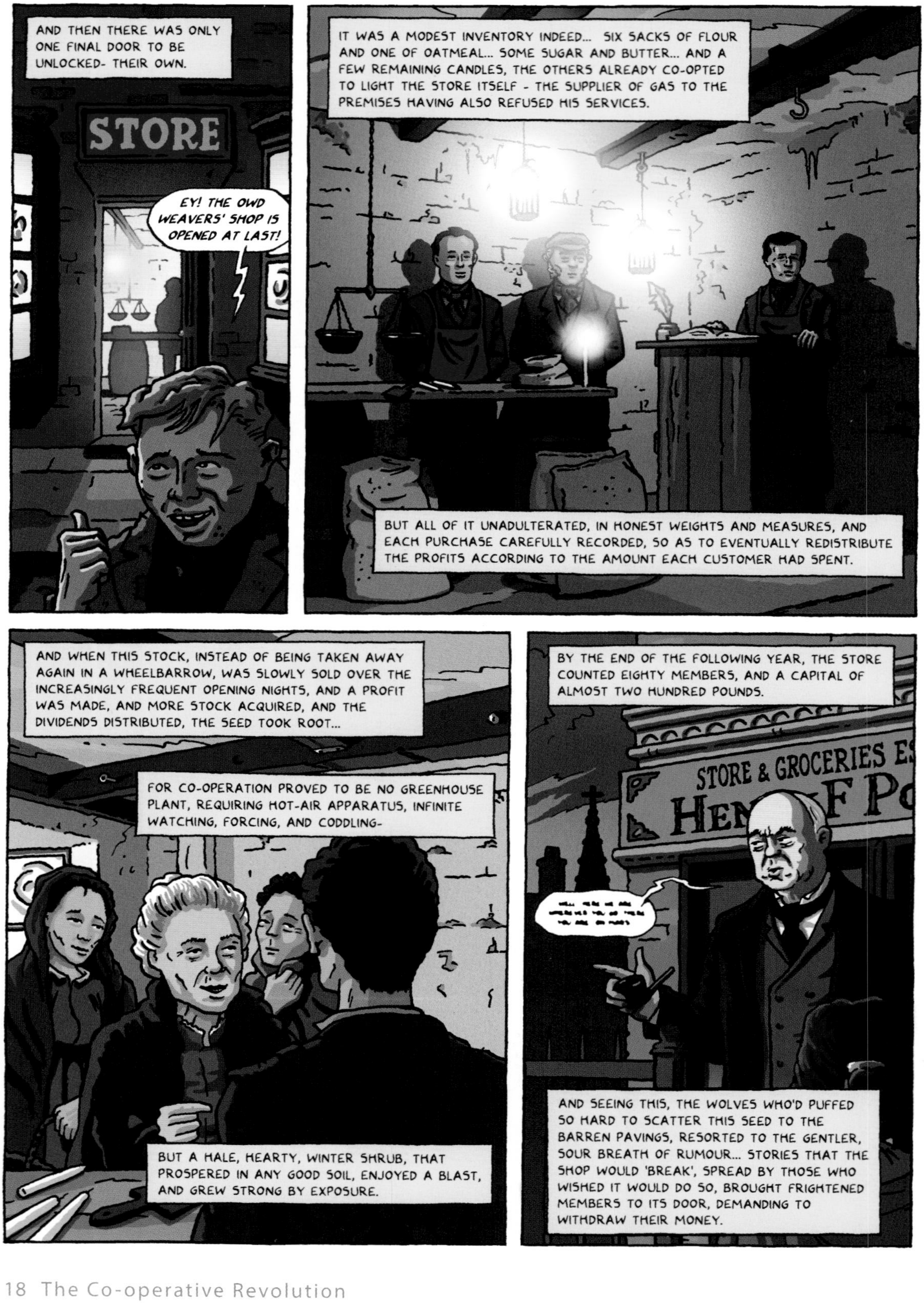
AND THEN THERE WAS ONLY ONE FINAL DOOR TO BE UNLOCKED- THEIR OWN.
STORE
EY! THE OWD WEAVERS' SHOP IS OPENED AT LAST!
IT WAS A MODEST INVENTORY INDEED... SIX SACKS OF FLOUR AND ONE OF OATMEAL... SOME SUGAR AND BUTTER... AND A FEW REMAINING CANDLES, THE OTHERS ALREADY CO-OPTED TO LIGHT THE STORE ITSELF - THE SUPPLIER OF GAS TO THE PREMISES HAVING ALSO REFUSED HIS SERVICES.
BUT ALL OF IT UNADULTERATED, IN HONEST WEIGHTS AND MEASURES, AND EACH PURCHASE CAREFULLY RECORDED, SO AS TO EVENTUALLY REDISTRIBUTE THE PROFITS ACCORDING TO THE AMOUNT EACH CUSTOMER HAD SPENT.
AND WHEN THIS STOCK, INSTEAD OF BEING TAKEN AWAY AGAIN IN A WHEELBARROW, WAS SLOWLY SOLD OVER THE INCREASINGLY FREQUENT OPENING NIGHTS, AND A PROFIT WAS MADE, AND MORE STOCK ACQUIRED, AND THE DIVIDENDS DISTRIBUTED, THE SEED TOOK ROOT...
FOR CO-OPERATION PROVED TO BE NO GREENHOUSE PLANT, REQUIRING HOT-AIR APPARATUS, INFINITE WATCHING, FORCING, AND CODDLING-
BUT A HALE, HEARTY, WINTER SHRUB, THAT PROSPERED IN ANY GOOD SOIL, ENJOYED A BLAST, AND GREW STRONG BY EXPOSURE.
BY THE END OF THE FOLLOWING YEAR, THE STORE COUNTED EIGHTY MEMBERS, AND A CAPITAL OF ALMOST TWO HUNDRED POUNDS.
STORE & GROCERIES
AND SEEING THIS, THE WOLVES WHO'D PUFFED SO HARD TO SCATTER THIS SEED TO THE BARREN PAVINGS, RESORTED TO THE GENTLER, SOUR BREATH OF RUMOUR... STORIES THAT THE SHOP WOULD 'BREAK', SPREAD BY THOSE WHO WISHED IT WOULD DO SO, BROUGHT FRIGHTENED MEMBERS TO ITS DOOR, DEMANDING TO WITHDRAW THEIR MONEY.

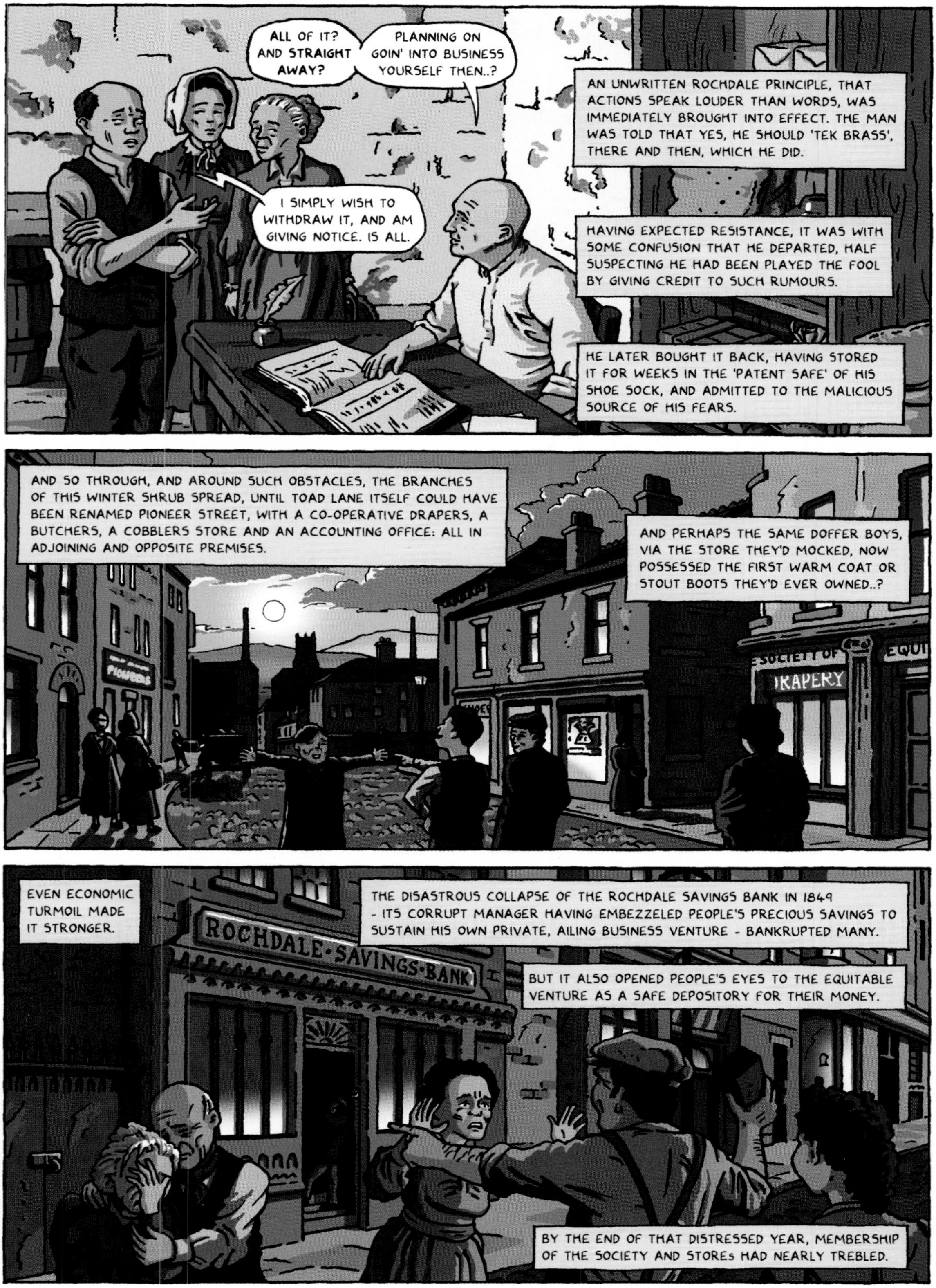
ALL OF IT? AND STRAIGHT AWAY?
PLANNING ON GOIN' INTO BUSINESS YOURSELF THEN..?
I SIMPLY WISH TO WITHDRAW IT, AND AM GIVING NOTICE. IS ALL.
AN UNWRITTEN ROCHDALE PRINCIPLE, THAT ACTIONS SPEAK LOUDER THAN WORDS, WAS IMMEDIATELY BROUGHT INTO EFFECT. THE MAN WAS TOLD THAT YES, HE SHOULD 'TEK BRASS', THERE AND THEN, WHICH HE DID.
HAVING EXPECTED RESISTANCE, IT WAS WITH SOME CONFUSION THAT HE DEPARTED, HALF SUSPECTING HE HAD BEEN PLAYED THE FOOL BY GIVING CREDIT TO SUCH RUMOURS.
HE LATER BOUGHT IT BACK, HAVING STORED IT FOR WEEKS IN THE 'PATENT SAFE' OF HIS SHOE SOCK, AND ADMITTED TO THE MALICIOUS SOURCE OF HIS FEARS.
AND SO THROUGH, AND AROUND SUCH OBSTACLES, THE BRANCHES OF THIS WINTER SHRUB SPREAD, UNTIL TOAD LANE ITSELF COULD HAVE BEEN RENAMED PIONEER STREET, WITH A CO-OPERATIVE DRAPERS, A BUTCHERS, A COBBLERS STORE AND AN ACCOUNTING OFFICE: ALL IN ADJOINING AND OPPOSITE PREMISES.
AND PERHAPS THE SAME DOFFER BOYS, VIA THE STORE THEY'D MOCKED, NOW POSSESSED THE FIRST WARM COAT OR STOUT BOOTS THEY'D EVER OWNED..?
PIONEERS
SOCIETY OF
EQUI
DRAPERY
EVEN ECONOMIC TURMOIL MADE IT STRONGER.
THE DISASTROUS COLLAPSE OF THE ROCHDALE SAVINGS BANK IN 1849 - ITS CORRUPT MANAGER HAVING EMBEZZELED PEOPLE'S PRECIOUS SAVINGS TO SUSTAIN HIS OWN PRIVATE, AILING BUSINESS VENTURE - BANKRUPTED MANY.
ROCHDALE·SAVINGS·BANK
BUT IT ALSO OPENED PEOPLE'S EYES TO THE EQUITABLE VENTURE AS A SAFE DEPOSITORY FOR THEIR MONEY.
BY THE END OF THAT DISTRESSED YEAR, MEMBERSHIP OF THE SOCIETY AND STORES HAD NEARLY TREBLED.

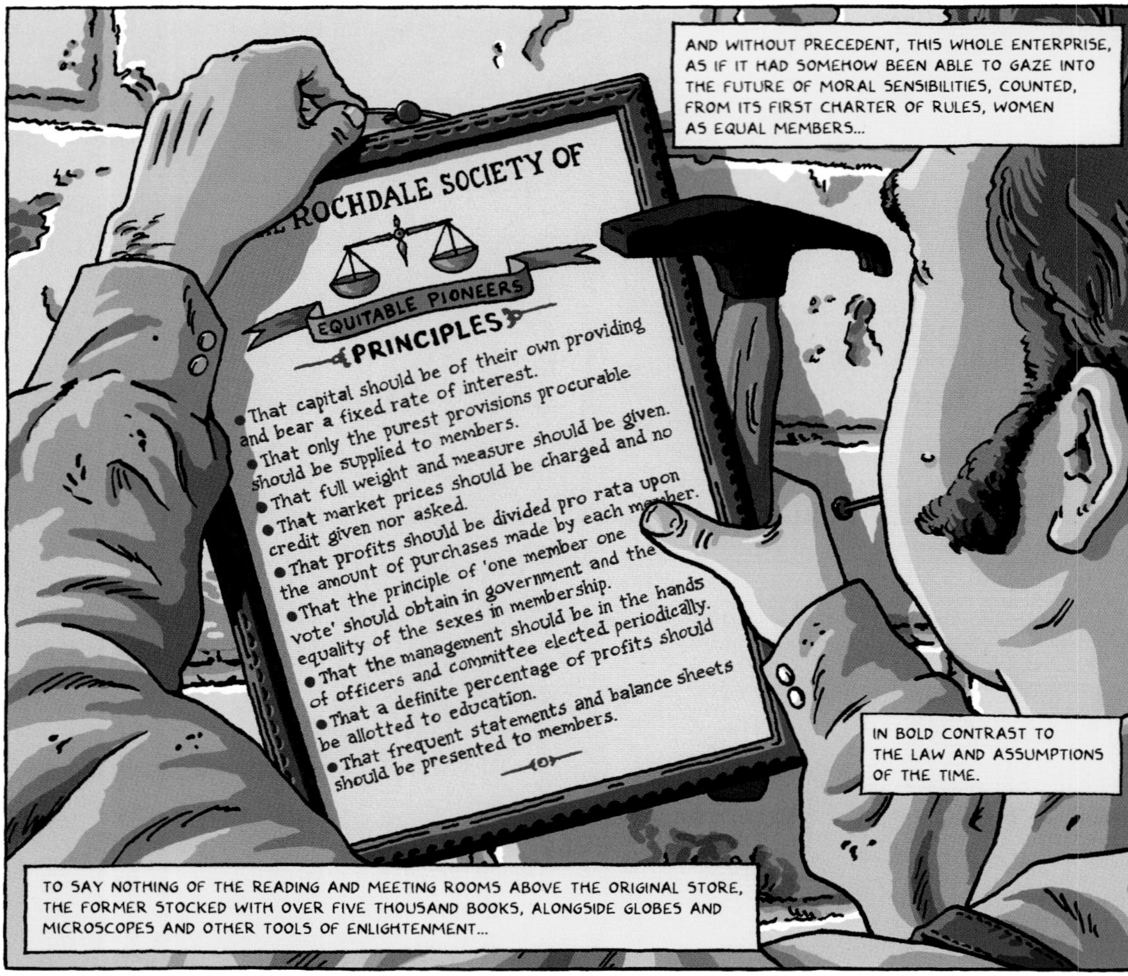
AND WITHOUT PRECEDENT, THIS WHOLE ENTERPRISE, AS IF IT HAD SOMEHOW BEEN ABLE TO GAZE INTO THE FUTURE OF MORAL SENSIBILITIES, COUNTED, FROM ITS FIRST CHARTER OF RULES, WOMEN AS EQUAL MEMBERS...
ROCHDALE SOCIETY OF
EQUITABLE PIONEERS
PRINCIPLES
• That capital should be of their own providing and bear a fixed rate of interest.
• That only the purest provisions procurable should be supplied to members.
• That full weight and measure should be given.
• That market prices should be charged and no credit given nor asked.
• That profits should be divided pro rata upon the amount of purchases made by each
• That the principle of 'one member one vote' should obtain in government and the equality of the sexes in membership.
• That the management should be in the hands of officers and committee elected periodically.
• That a definite percentage of profits should be allotted to education.
• That frequent statements and balance sheets should be presented to members.
IN BOLD CONTRAST TO THE LAW AND ASSUMPTIONS OF THE TIME.
TO SAY NOTHING OF THE READING AND MEETING ROOMS ABOVE THE ORIGINAL STORE, THE FORMER STOCKED WITH OVER FIVE THOUSAND BOOKS, ALONGSIDE GLOBES AND MICROSCOPES AND OTHER TOOLS OF ENLIGHTENMENT...

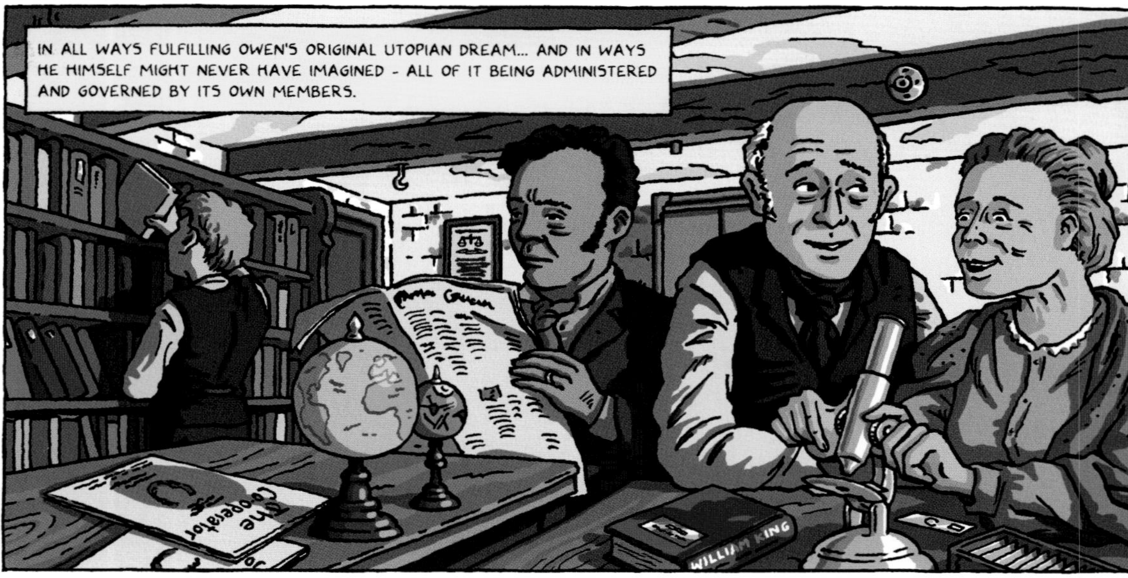
IN ALL WAYS FULFILLING OWEN'S ORIGINAL UTOPIAN DREAM... AND IN WAYS HE HIMSELF MIGHT NEVER HAVE IMAGINED - ALL OF IT BEING ADMINISTERED AND GOVERNED BY ITS OWN MEMBERS.
The Cooperator
WILLIAM KING

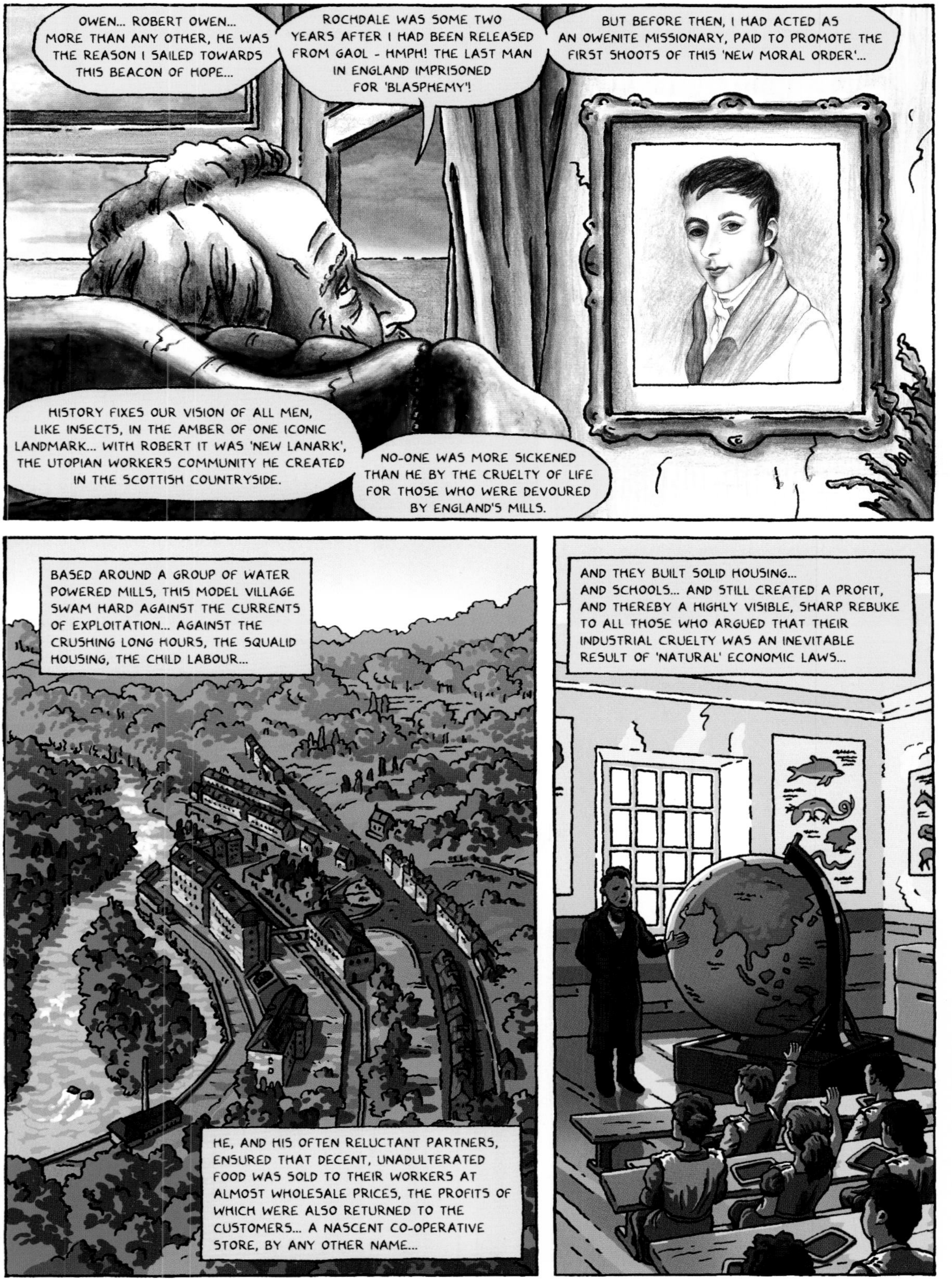
OWEN... ROBERT OWEN... MORE THAN ANY OTHER, HE WAS THE REASON I SAILED TOWARDS THIS BEACON OF HOPE...
ROCHDALE WAS SOME TWO YEARS AFTER I HAD BEEN RELEASED FROM GAOL - HMPH! THE LAST MAN IN ENGLAND IMPRISONED FOR 'BLASPHEMY'!
BUT BEFORE THEN, I HAD ACTED AS AN OWENITE MISSIONARY, PAID TO PROMOTE THE FIRST SHOOTS OF THIS 'NEW MORAL ORDER'...
HISTORY FIXES OUR VISION OF ALL MEN, LIKE INSECTS, IN THE AMBER OF ONE ICONIC LANDMARK... WITH ROBERT IT WAS 'NEW LANARK', THE UTOPIAN WORKERS COMMUNITY HE CREATED IN THE SCOTTISH COUNTRYSIDE.
NO-ONE WAS MORE SICKENED THAN HE BY THE CRUELTY OF LIFE FOR THOSE WHO WERE DEVOURED BY ENGLAND'S MILLS.
BASED AROUND A GROUP OF WATER POWERED MILLS, THIS MODEL VILLAGE SWAM HARD AGAINST THE CURRENTS OF EXPLOITATION... AGAINST THE CRUSHING LONG HOURS, THE SQUALID HOUSING, THE CHILD LABOUR...
HE, AND HIS OFTEN RELUCTANT PARTNERS, ENSURED THAT DECENT, UNADULTERATED FOOD WAS SOLD TO THEIR WORKERS AT ALMOST WHOLESALE PRICES, THE PROFITS OF WHICH WERE ALSO RETURNED TO THE CUSTOMERS... A NASCENT CO-OPERATIVE STORE, BY ANY OTHER NAME...
AND THEY BUILT SOLID HOUSING... AND SCHOOLS... AND STILL CREATED A PROFIT, AND THEREBY A HIGHLY VISIBLE, SHARP REBUKE TO ALL THOSE WHO ARGUED THAT THEIR INDUSTRIAL CRUELTY WAS AN INEVITABLE RESULT OF 'NATURAL' ECONOMIC LAWS...

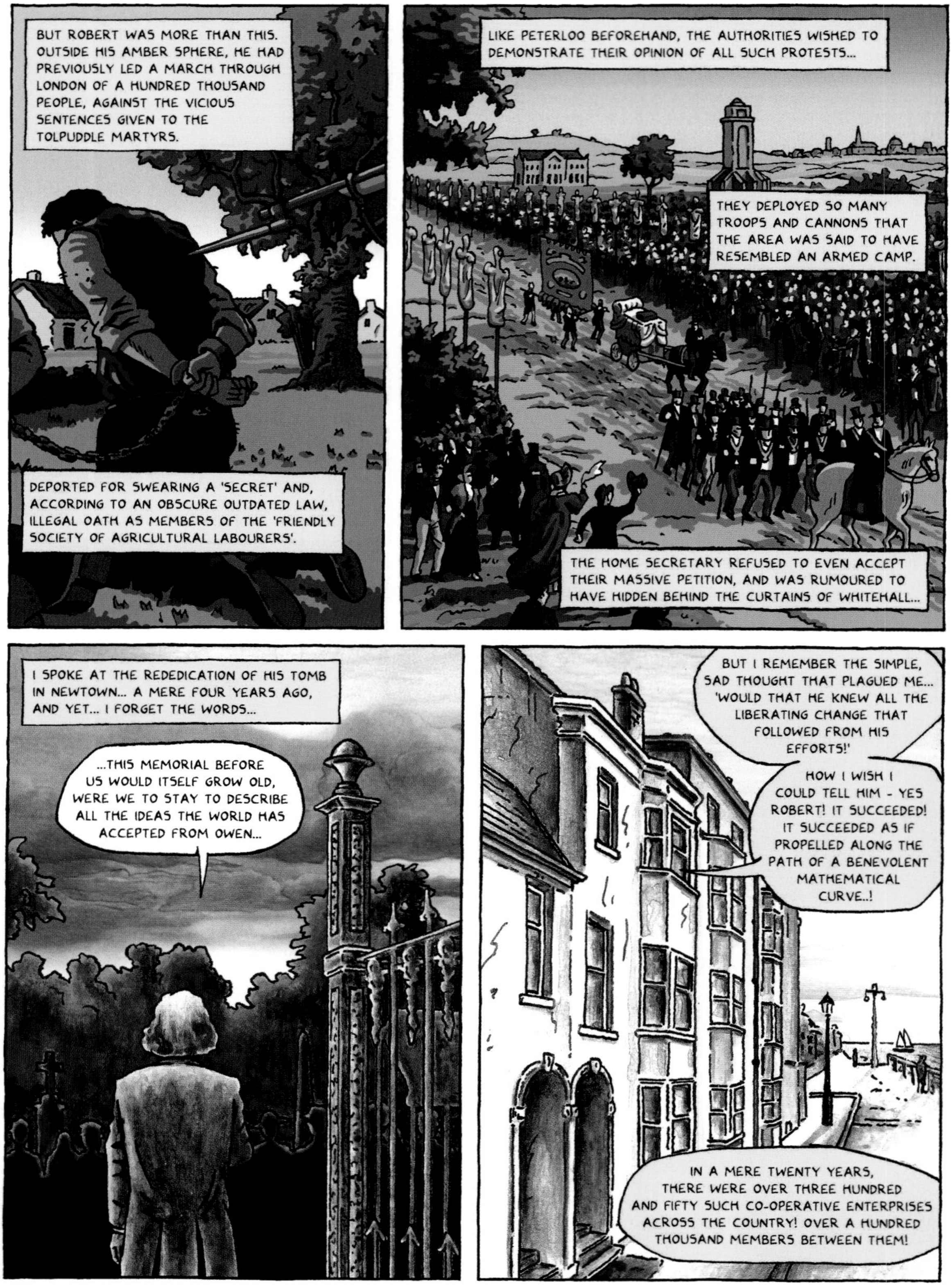
BUT ROBERT WAS MORE THAN THIS. OUTSIDE HIS AMBER SPHERE, HE HAD PREVIOUSLY LED A MARCH THROUGH LONDON OF A HUNDRED THOUSAND PEOPLE, AGAINST THE VICIOUS SENTENCES GIVEN TO THE TOLPUDDLE MARTYRS.
DEPORTED FOR SWEARING A 'SECRET' AND, ACCORDING TO AN OBSCURE OUTDATED LAW, ILLEGAL OATH AS MEMBERS OF THE 'FRIENDLY SOCIETY OF AGRICULTURAL LABOURERS'.
LIKE PETERLOO BEFOREHAND, THE AUTHORITIES WISHED TO DEMONSTRATE THEIR OPINION OF ALL SUCH PROTESTS...
THEY DEPLOYED SO MANY TROOPS AND CANNONS THAT THE AREA WAS SAID TO HAVE RESEMBLED AN ARMED CAMP.
THE HOME SECRETARY REFUSED TO EVEN ACCEPT THEIR MASSIVE PETITION, AND WAS RUMOURED TO HAVE HIDDEN BEHIND THE CURTAINS OF WHITEHALL...
I SPOKE AT THE REDEDICATION OF HIS TOMB IN NEWTOWN... A MERE FOUR YEARS AGO, AND YET... I FORGET THE WORDS...
...THIS MEMORIAL BEFORE US WOULD ITSELF GROW OLD, WERE WE TO STAY TO DESCRIBE ALL THE IDEAS THE WORLD HAS ACCEPTED FROM OWEN...
BUT I REMEMBER THE SIMPLE, SAD THOUGHT THAT PLAGUED ME... 'WOULD THAT HE KNEW ALL THE LIBERATING CHANGE THAT FOLLOWED FROM HIS EFFORTS!'
HOW I WISH I COULD TELL HIM - YES ROBERT! IT SUCCEEDED! IT SUCCEEDED AS IF PROPELLED ALONG THE PATH OF A BENEVOLENT MATHEMATICAL CURVE..!
IN A MERE TWENTY YEARS, THERE WERE OVER THREE HUNDRED AND FIFTY SUCH CO-OPERATIVE ENTERPRISES ACROSS THE COUNTRY! OVER A HUNDRED THOUSAND MEMBERS BETWEEN THEM!

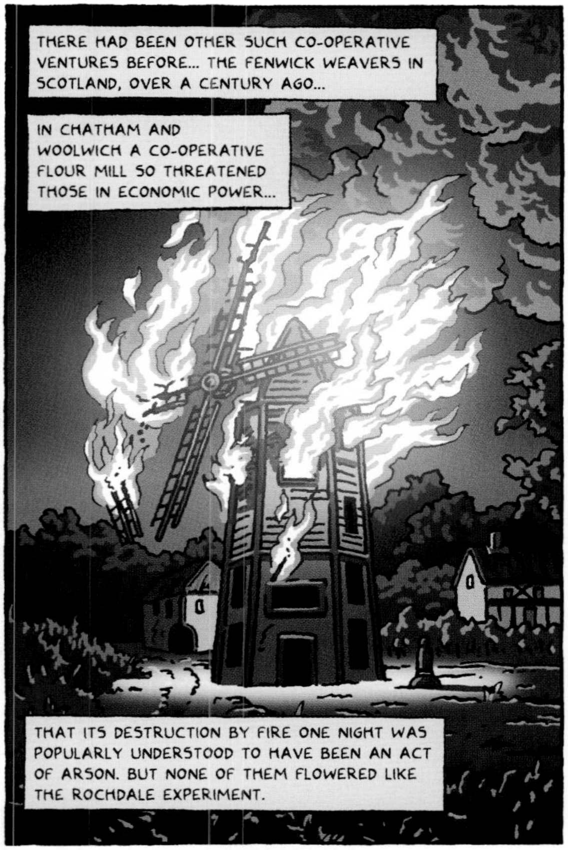
THERE HAD BEEN OTHER SUCH CO-OPERATIVE VENTURES BEFORE... THE FENWICK WEAVERS IN SCOTLAND, OVER A CENTURY AGO...
IN CHATHAM AND WOOLWICH A CO-OPERATIVE FLOUR MILL SO THREATENED THOSE IN ECONOMIC POWER...
THAT ITS DESTRUCTION BY FIRE ONE NIGHT WAS POPULARLY UNDERSTOOD TO HAVE BEEN AN ACT OF ARSON. BUT NONE OF THEM FLOWERED LIKE THE ROCHDALE EXPERIMENT.

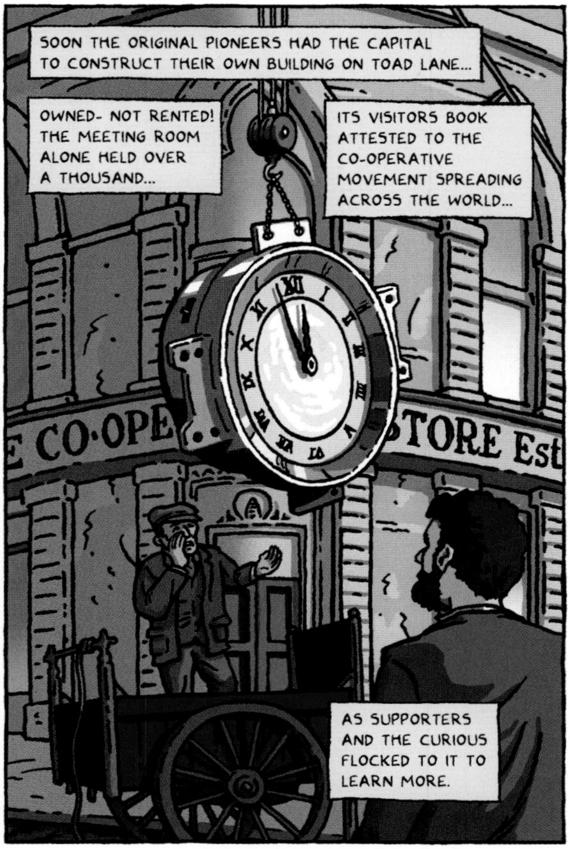
SOON THE ORIGINAL PIONEERS HAD THE CAPITAL TO CONSTRUCT THEIR OWN BUILDING ON TOAD LANE...
OWNED- NOT RENTED! THE MEETING ROOM ALONE HELD OVER A THOUSAND...
ITS VISITORS BOOK ATTESTED TO THE CO-OPERATIVE MOVEMENT SPREADING ACROSS THE WORLD...
CO-OPE
STORE Est
AS SUPPORTERS AND THE CURIOUS FLOCKED TO IT TO LEARN MORE.

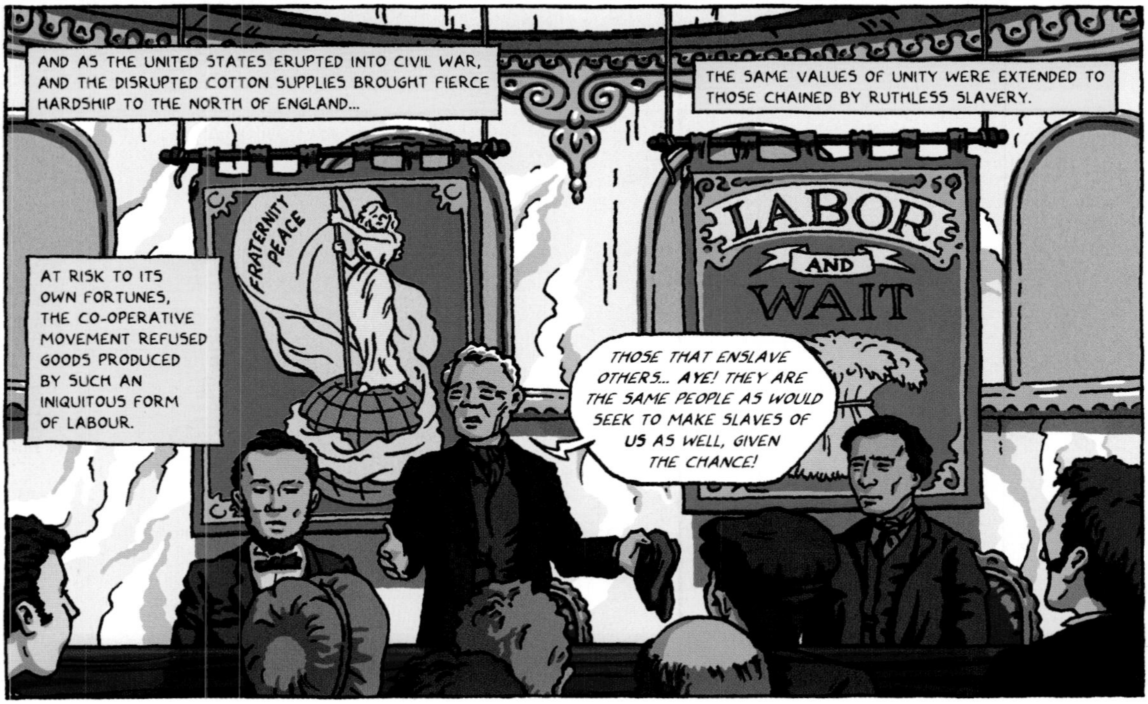
AND AS THE UNITED STATES ERUPTED INTO CIVIL WAR, AND THE DISRUPTED COTTON SUPPLIES BROUGHT FIERCE HARDSHIP TO THE NORTH OF ENGLAND...
THE SAME VALUES OF UNITY WERE EXTENDED TO THOSE CHAINED BY RUTHLESS SLAVERY.
FRATERNITY PEACE
LABOR AND WAIT
AT RISK TO ITS OWN FORTUNES, THE CO-OPERATIVE MOVEMENT REFUSED GOODS PRODUCED BY SUCH AN INIQUITOUS FORM OF LABOUR.
THOSE THAT ENSLAVE OTHERS... AYE! THEY ARE THE SAME PEOPLE AS WOULD SEEK TO MAKE SLAVES OF US AS WELL, GIVEN THE CHANCE!

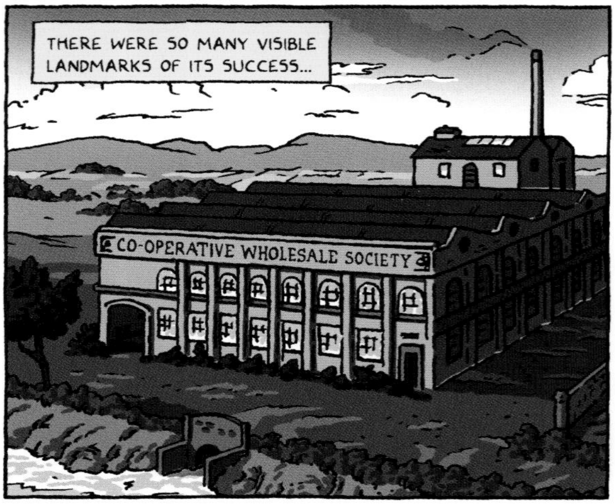
THERE WERE SO MANY VISIBLE LANDMARKS OF ITS SUCCESS...
CO-OPERATIVE WHOLESALE SOCIETY

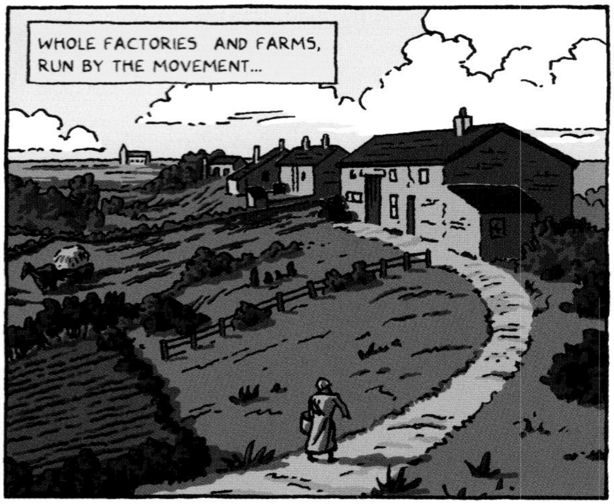
WHOLE FACTORIES AND FARMS, RUN BY THE MOVEMENT...

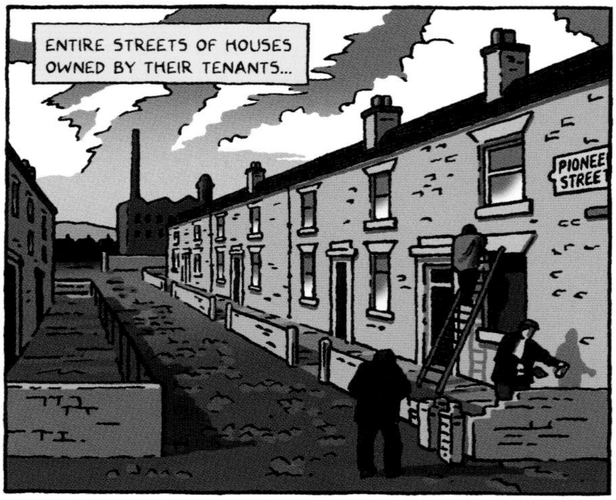
ENTIRE STREETS OF HOUSES OWNED BY THEIR TENANTS...

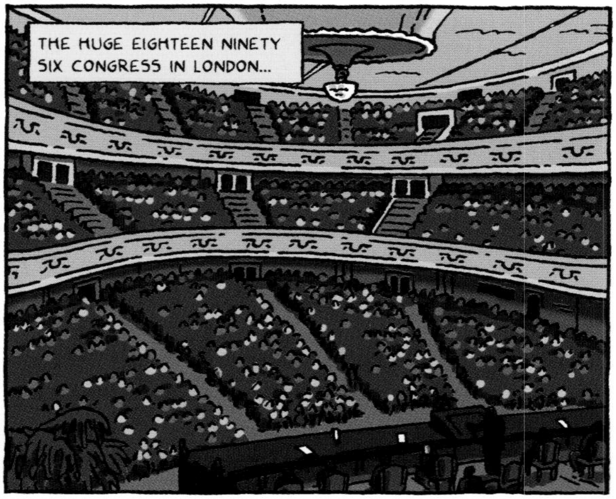
THE HUGE EIGHTEEN NINETY SIX CONGRESS IN LONDON...

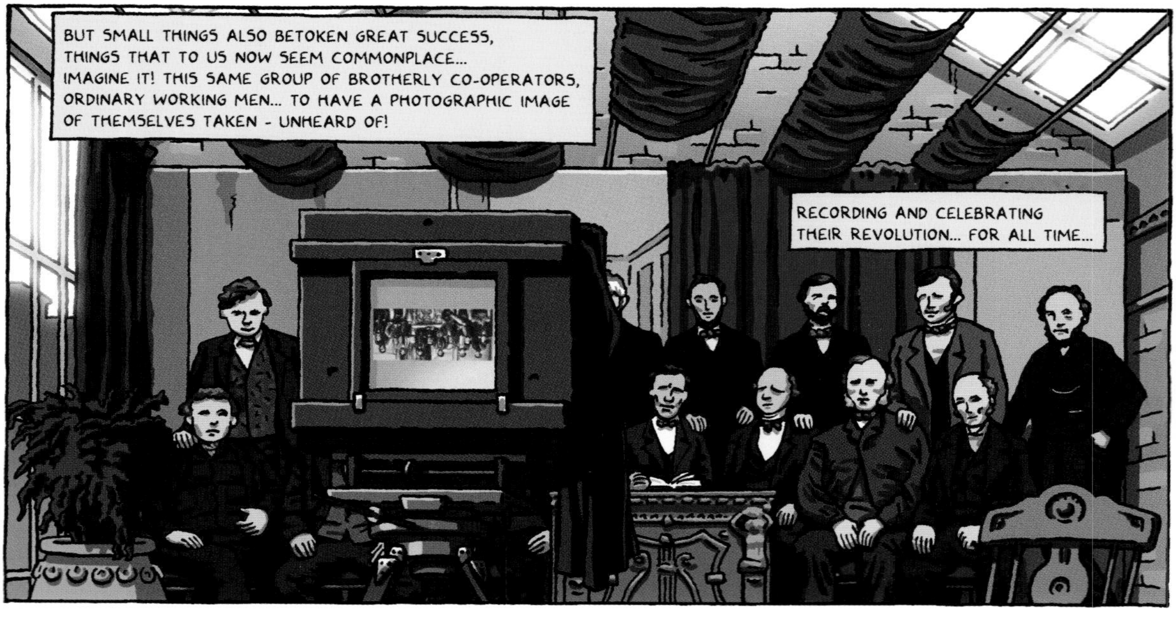
BUT SMALL THINGS ALSO BETOKEN GREAT SUCCESS, THINGS THAT TO US NOW SEEM COMMONPLACE... IMAGINE IT! THIS SAME GROUP OF BROTHERLY CO-OPERATORS, ORDINARY WORKING MEN... TO HAVE A PHOTOGRAPHIC IMAGE OF THEMSELVES TAKEN - UNHEARD OF!
RECORDING AND CELEBRATING THEIR REVOLUTION... FOR ALL TIME...

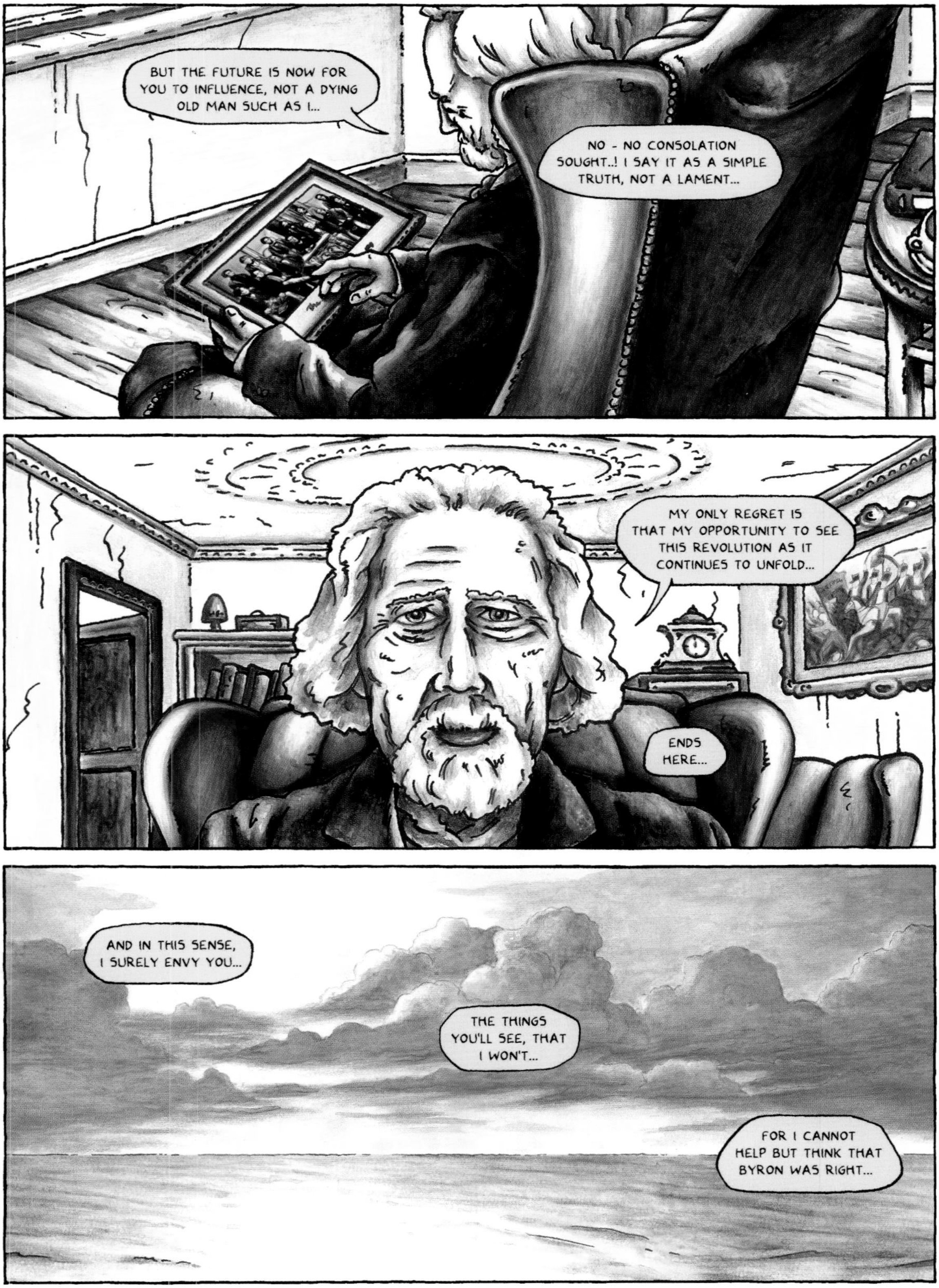
BUT THE FUTURE IS NOW FOR YOU TO INFLUENCE, NOT A DYING OLD MAN SUCH AS I...
NO - NO CONSOLATION SOUGHT..! I SAY IT AS A SIMPLE TRUTH, NOT A LAMENT...
MY ONLY REGRET IS THAT MY OPPORTUNITY TO SEE THIS REVOLUTION AS IT CONTINUES TO UNFOLD...
ENDS HERE...
AND IN THIS SENSE, I SURELY ENVY YOU...
THE THINGS YOU'LL SEE, THAT I WON'T...
FOR I CANNOT HELP BUT THINK THAT BYRON WAS RIGHT...

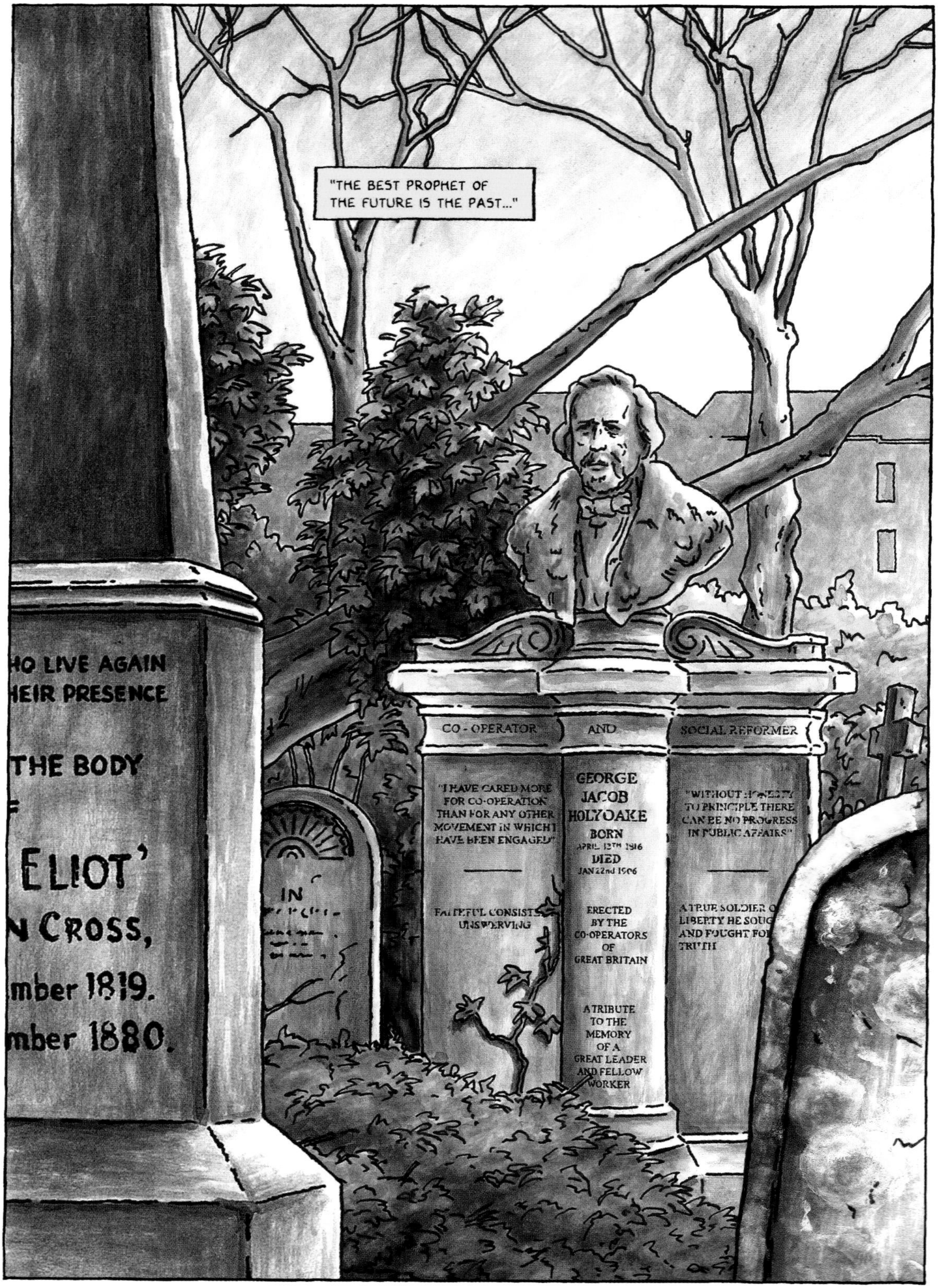
"THE BEST PROPHET OF THE FUTURE IS THE PAST..."
CO-OPERATOR
AND
SOCIAL REFORMER
"I HAVE CARED MORE FOR CO-OPERATION THAN FOR ANY OTHER MOVEMENT IN WHICH I HAVE BEEN ENGAGED"
GEORGE JACOB HOLYOAKE
BORN
DIED
ERECTED BY THE CO-OPERATORS OF GREAT BRITAIN
A TRIBUTE TO THE MEMORY OF A GREAT LEADER AND FELLOW WORKER
THE BODY
ELIOT'

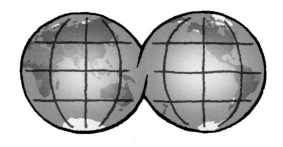

Today

THE CO-OPERATIVE MOVEMENT IS THE MOST durable and powerful grassroots movement the world has ever seen. It now has nearly one billion members worldwide.

In the UK, the co-operative economy has grown by a fifth since the financial crisis of 2008 – and this at a time when the rest of the UK economy has shrunk.

The UK mutuals sector has over 18,000 organizations, including co-operatives, building societies, housing associations, credit unions, insurers, clubs, societies, NHS Trusts and employee-owned businesses. The sector sustains a million jobs and has an annual turnover of over £111 billion ($178 billion).

The Emilia Romagna region, one of the wealthiest in Italy, is home to 8,100 co-operatives, the majority of which are agricultural, and together produce 40% of the region's GDP.

In the US, 900 rural electricity co-operatives deliver electricity to 42 million people in 47 states, making up 42% of the US's electric distribution lines and covering 75% of the land mass.

Canadian co-operatives produce 35% of the world's maple sugar.

The largest consumer co-ops in the world are in Japan, where one in three families and 91% of all farmers are members of a co-operative.

In India, over 239 million people are members of a co-operative.

Over 100 million people are employed by co-operatives across the world.

All in all, there are 1.4 million co-operatives on the planet – and overleaf is just a tiny sample of them...

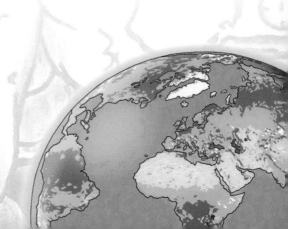

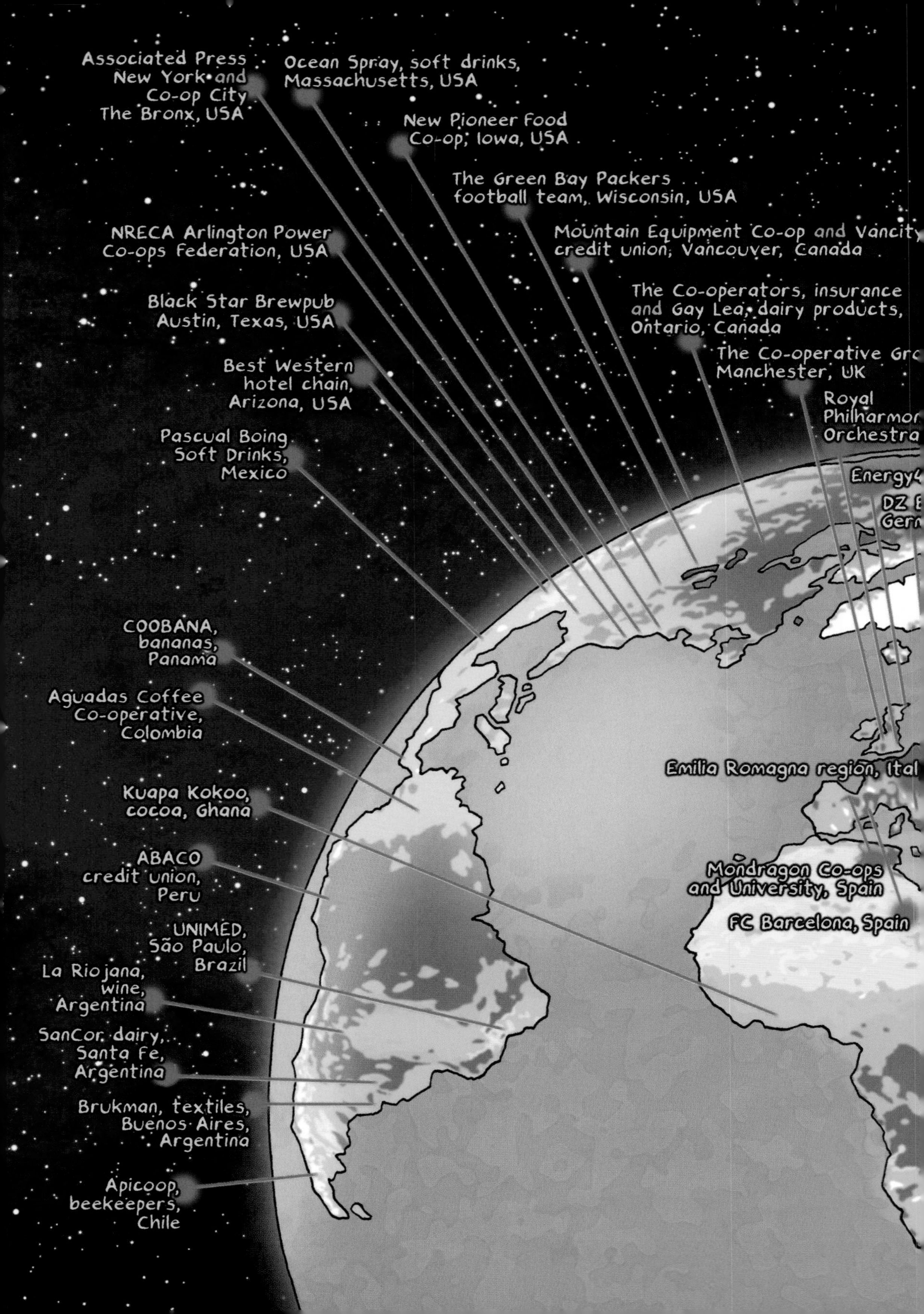
Associated Press New York and Co-op City The Bronx, USA
Ocean Spray, soft drinks, Massachusetts, USA
New Pioneer Food Co-op, Iowa, USA
The Green Bay Packers football team, Wisconsin, USA
NRECA Arlington Power Co-ops Federation, USA
Mountain Equipment Co-op and Vancity credit union, Vancouver, Canada
Black Star Brewpub Austin, Texas, USA
The Co-operators, insurance and Gay Lea, dairy products, Ontario, Canada
Best Western hotel chain, Arizona, USA
The Co-operative Gro
Manchester, UK
Royal Philharmon
Orchestra
Pascual Boing Soft Drinks, Mexico
Energy4
DZ B
Germ
COOBANA, bananas, Panama
Aguadas Coffee Co-operative, Colombia
Emilia Romagna region, Ital
Kuapa Kokoo, cocoa, Ghana
ABACO credit union, Peru
Mondragon Co-ops and University, Spain
FC Barcelona, Spain
UNIMED, São Paulo, Brazil
La Riojana, wine, Argentina
SanCor dairy, Santa Fe, Argentina
Brukman, textiles, Buenos Aires, Argentina
Apicoop, beekeepers, Chile

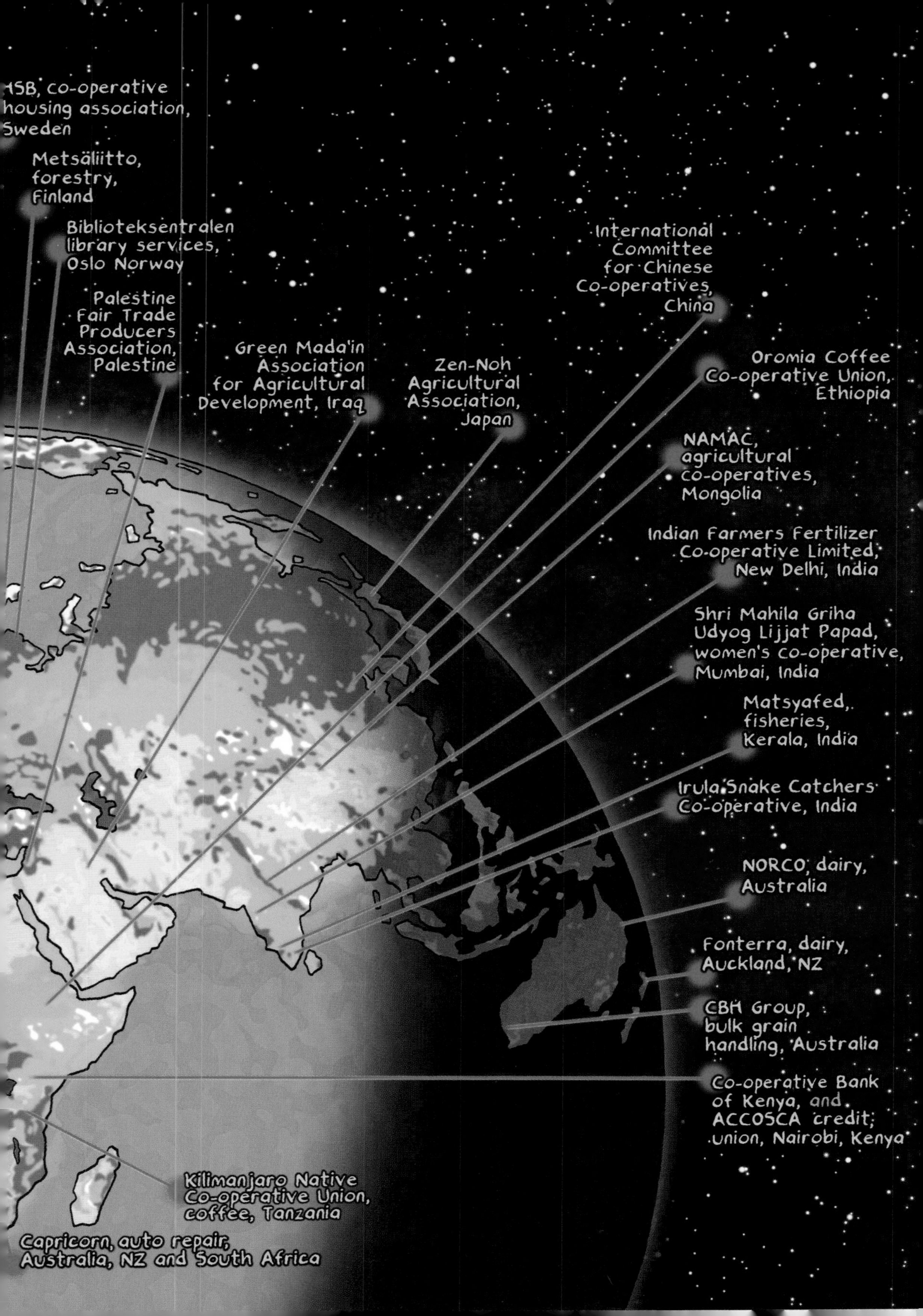
HSB, co-operative housing association, Sweden
Metsäliitto, forestry, Finland
Biblioteksentralen library services, Oslo Norway
Palestine Fair Trade Producers Association, Palestine
Green Mada'in Association for Agricultural Development, Iraq
Zen-Noh Agricultural Association, Japan
International Committee for Chinese Co-operatives, China
Oromia Coffee Co-operative Union, Ethiopia
NAMAC, agricultural co-operatives, Mongolia
Indian Farmers Fertilizer Co-operative Limited, New Delhi, India
Shri Mahila Griha Udyog Lijjat Papad, women's co-operative, Mumbai, India
Matsyafed, fisheries, Kerala, India
Irula Snake Catchers Co-operative, India
NORCO, dairy, Australia
Fonterra, dairy, Auckland, NZ
CBH Group, bulk grain handling, Australia
Co-operative Bank of Kenya, and ACCOSCA credit union, Nairobi, Kenya
Kilimanjaro Native Co-operative Union, coffee, Tanzania
Capricorn, auto repair, Australia, NZ and South Africa

Co-op City, New York

ONE OF THE WORLD'S LARGEST housing co-operatives is located in New York – Co-op City, in the Bronx. Built on the 300-acre site of the defunct 'Freedomland' amusement park, it is home to approximately 60,000 residents.

It has 35 high-rise blocks and 240 townhouses, along with 12 places of worship, 10 schools, six nurseries, three shopping centres, several dental practices and its own subway stations..

It even has its own police force, which is 89 officers strong – the Co-op City Department of Public Safety (CCDP).

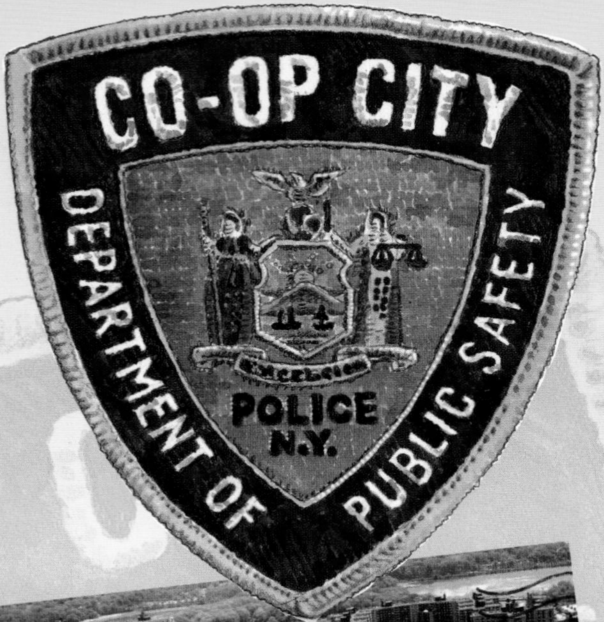
CO-OP CITY
DEPARTMENT OF PUBLIC SAFETY
POLICE
N.Y.

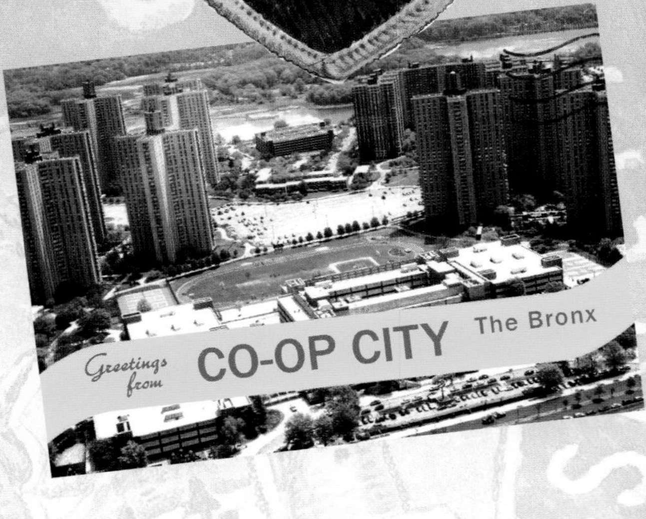
Greetings from
CO-OP CITY
The Bronx

'Strange, isn't it? Each man's life touches so many other lives. When he isn't around he leaves an awful hole, doesn't he?'

Clarence Oddbody in
It's a Wonderful Life (1946)

'Quite apart from our desire to avoid destroying the planet or economic meltdown, I offer another reason to position co-operation at the heart of our political economy: it will mean we are more likely to live sane, fruitful lives.'

Oliver James, psychologist, author and broadcaster (contemporary)

The snake catchers

THE IRULAS ARE AN INDIGENOUS FOREST-dwelling people in India, who traditionally made a living by catching snakes for their skins. Using nothing more than bare hands and a crowbar to dig the soil, the villagers captured deadly species such as cobras, vipers and kraits. However, when the Indian Parliament adopted new conservation laws in 1972, the Irulas' livelihood became illegal and punishable with jail.

Many felt it was the end of the road for this highly skilled people – some became farm labourers, others migrated to the urban shantytowns in search of jobs. But a small group formed the Irula Snake Catchers' Industrial Co-operative Society.

The snakes that the Irulas catch are taken to the co-operative's venom extraction centre, near Mamallapuram in Tamil Nadu, where they are milked for their venom and then released back into the wild. The Irulas are now the only suppliers of snake venom to laboratories across India, which use it in the production of life-saving anti-venom serum. The co-operative has grown from 26 to more than 300 members. Today, snake catchers can earn several times more per live snake turned in for milking than they did previously for the skins of the snakes.

Ramajal, a member of the co-op, says it has produced enormous benefits for her and her family: 'From the co-operative we get money, and we also get a bonus for every snake that we catch. The bonus means we can buy better food, and it helps with the children's education.'

'No man is an island entire of itself; every man is a piece of the continent, a part of the main.'

John Donne, poet (1572-1631)

More than a football club

ONE OF THE WORLD'S MOST PRESTIGIOUS football clubs, FC Barcelona has no shareholders — it's owned and democratically controlled by its 180,000 members.

Speaking at an international football conference, its elected president, Sandro Rosell, emphasized: 'Barcelona is not a business, it is a feeling. We are not owned by anybody, we are an association; we do not have "clients". I will never put a game on at 12 noon for the Chinese audience. We do want to open up our market but not to forget our roots. While I am the president, Barcelona will never, ever be for sale.'

Founded in 1899, the Catalan club has a long history of political rebellion. At a 1925 match the stadium crowd jeered the Spanish national anthem in protest at the military dictatorship of Miguel Primo de Rivera, who had recently seized power from the elected parliament. In punishment, the ground was closed for six months.

Players from FC Barcelona swiftly enlisted in the fight against the fascist military uprising led by Generalissimo Franco, and in 1936 Josep Sunyol, the then president, was murdered by soldiers loyal to the dictator.

Fans leaving the stadium in the pouring rain after a 1951 victory against Santander refused to catch the available trams as an act of solidarity with the local boycott, protesting a 40% increase in fares imposed by the local authorities under Franco's rule.

The club's motto 'Més que un club' (More than a club) reflects this proud tradition, and is emblazoned in huge letters across the stadium by its multi-coloured seats.

'There is but one mode by which man can possess in perpetuity all the happiness which his nature is capable of enjoying- that is by the union and co-operation of all for the benefit of each.'

Robert Owen, co-operative pioneer (1771-1858)

'How selfish soever man may be supposed, there are evidently some principles in his nature, which interest him in the fortunes of others, and render their happiness necessary to him, though he derives nothing from it, except the pleasure of seeing it.'

Adam Smith, economist (1723-1790)

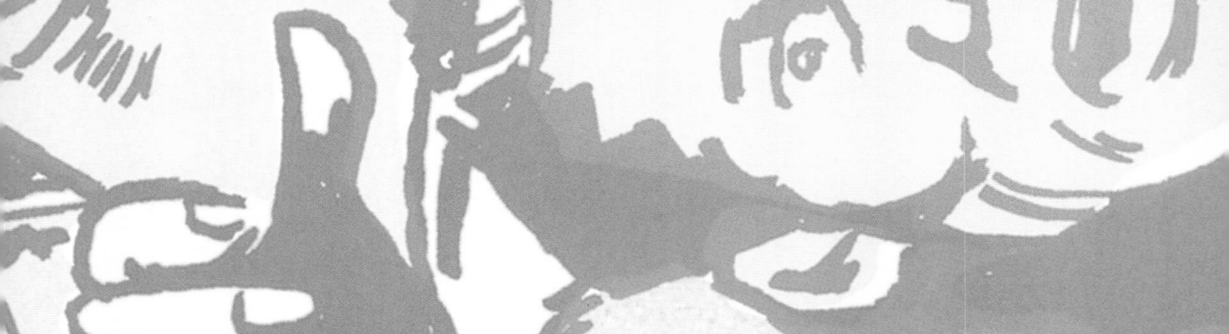

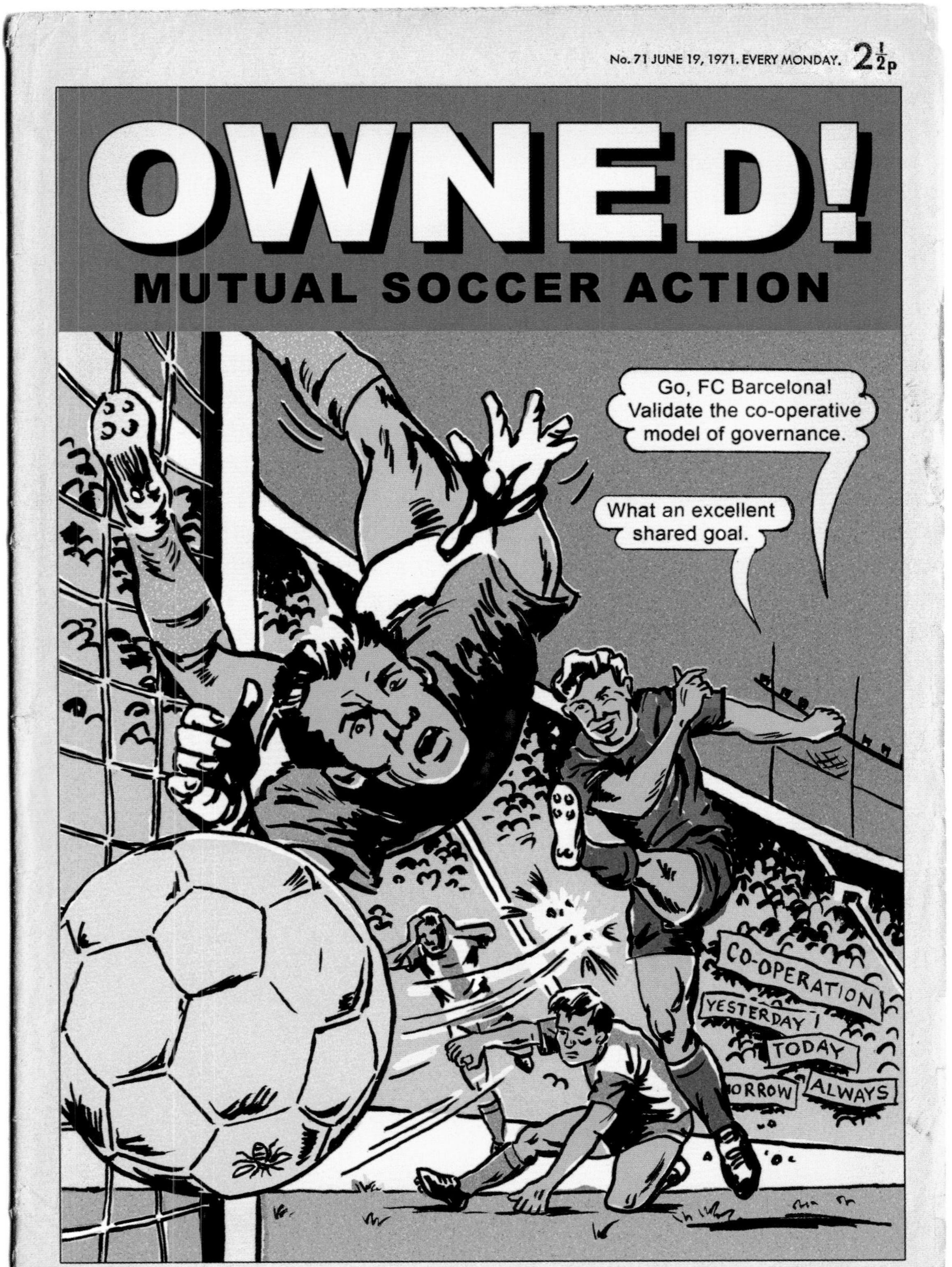
No. 71 JUNE 19, 1971. EVERY MONDAY. 2½p
OWNED!
MUTUAL SOCCER ACTION
Go, FC Barcelona! Validate the co-operative model of governance.
What an excellent shared goal.
CO-OPERATION
YESTERDAY
TODAY
ORROW
ALWAYS

Workers to the rescue

EXTRAORDINARY CHANGES CAME TO Argentina during the severe economic crisis that began in 1999, many of them defying cynical expectations of a collapse into 'dog eat dog' urban chaos. As well as reverting to moneyless systems of barter to survive the turmoil and unemployment, people took control of an estimated one hundred collapsed and bankrupt businesses, deciding to run them for themselves.

On 18 December 2001 the Brukman clothing manufacturing company in Buenos Aires was abandoned by its owners and closed, but 50 workers from the factory, mostly women, occupied the building overnight, and resumed production the next day. They slowly gathered new clients, paid off previous debts, and eventually took on 10 new members of staff.

The owners soon gained an eviction ruling, and the staff were confronted by over 300 armed soldiers, who forced them out of the building in the middle of the night. During the subsequent months, a protest camp was set up outside the premises and, despite subsequent attacks by the police using teargas, water cannons and rubber bullets, the protesters won. A 2003 ruling by the municipal council finally gave the '18 de Diciembre' Workers' Co-operative legal control of the factory, and it continues to trade on this basis today.

> 'At its heart, it is a story about how a revolution in human society that began with the rise of democracy in politics continues to unfold as the democratic idea struggles to find its place in the world of economics. If economic democracy is the hidden face of this ongoing revolution, then the history of the co-operative idea is its most durable expression.'
>
> **John Restakis**, author of *Humanizing the Economy*, contemporary

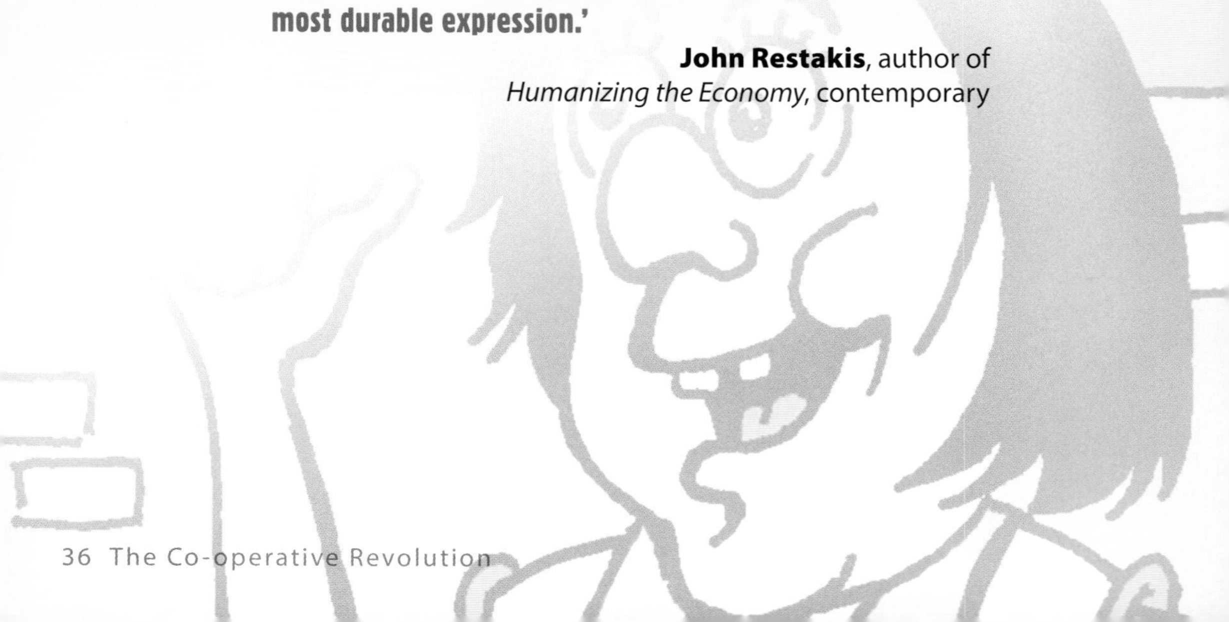

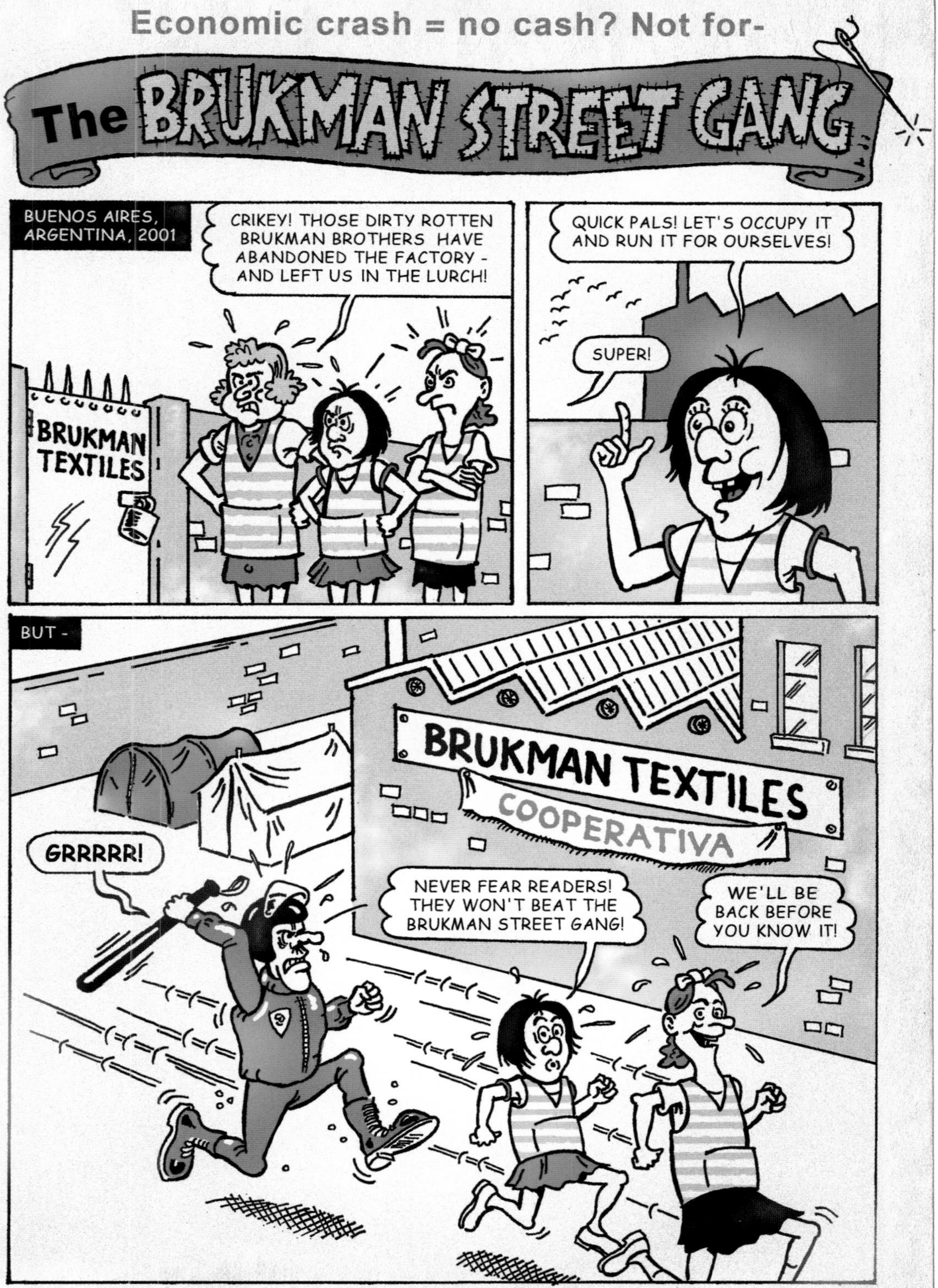
Economic crash = no cash? Not for-
The BRUKMAN STREET GANG
BUENOS AIRES, ARGENTINA, 2001
CRIKEY! THOSE DIRTY ROTTEN BRUKMAN BROTHERS HAVE ABANDONED THE FACTORY - AND LEFT US IN THE LURCH!
BRUKMAN TEXTILES
QUICK PALS! LET'S OCCUPY IT AND RUN IT FOR OURSELVES!
SUPER!
BUT -
BRUKMAN TEXTILES
COOPERATIVA
GRRRRR!
NEVER FEAR READERS! THEY WON'T BEAT THE BRUKMAN STREET GANG!
WE'LL BE BACK BEFORE YOU KNOW IT!

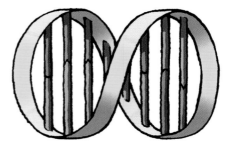

Always

SEEING RED

Throughout the history of evolutionary science, many have claimed that Darwin's observations about the 'survival of the fittest' somehow reinforce a particular interpretation of the world:

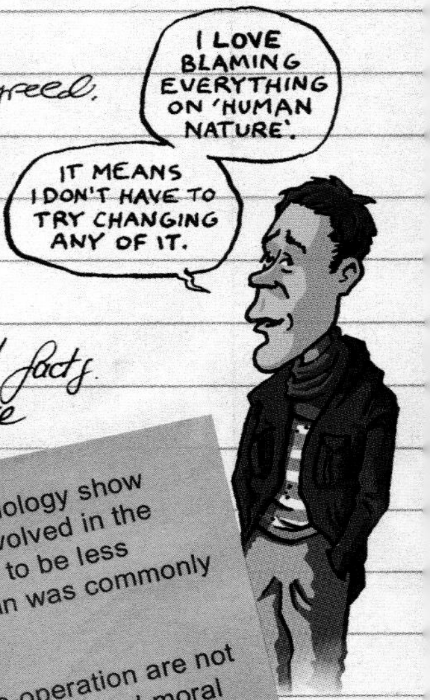

I LOVE BLAMING EVERYTHING ON 'HUMAN NATURE'.
IT MEANS I DON'T HAVE TO TRY CHANGING ANY OF IT.

1) That the default position of nature is one of pure self-interested greed.

2) That this means our society can only be successfully and efficiently run on the basis of fierce competition and selfishness

3) And that the idea of co-operation as a viable economic and political force therefore contradicts the 'natural order' of the world.

However, this twisted view of nature doesn't reflect the actual facts. Although selfishness and cruelty are major features of nature, there are other, equally powerful, co-operative forces at play.

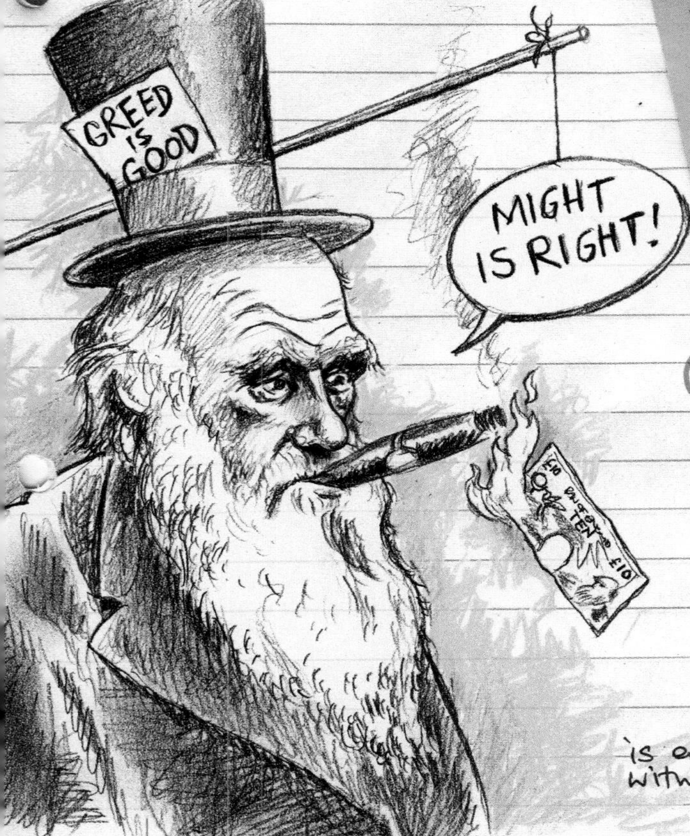

GREED IS GOOD
MIGHT IS RIGHT!

"New insights from biology show that humans have evolved in the struggle for survival to be less naturally selfish than was commonly believed.

Generosity and co-operation are not merely imposed by laws and moral codes. They spring from within, because in evolution, as in business, virtue pays dividends."

FT Editorial, 24th December 1996

Co-operation is:

1) Just as common as self-interest within natural systems

2) An efficient strategy for survival and success

3) And in many situations is even the best strategy to survive within the competitive arena of the natural world.

Despite being underestimated, neglected and dismissed, co-operation in nature is neither a novelty nor an exception to the rule and, over the last twenty years, a revolution within the scientific community has been turning that traditional assumption on its head.

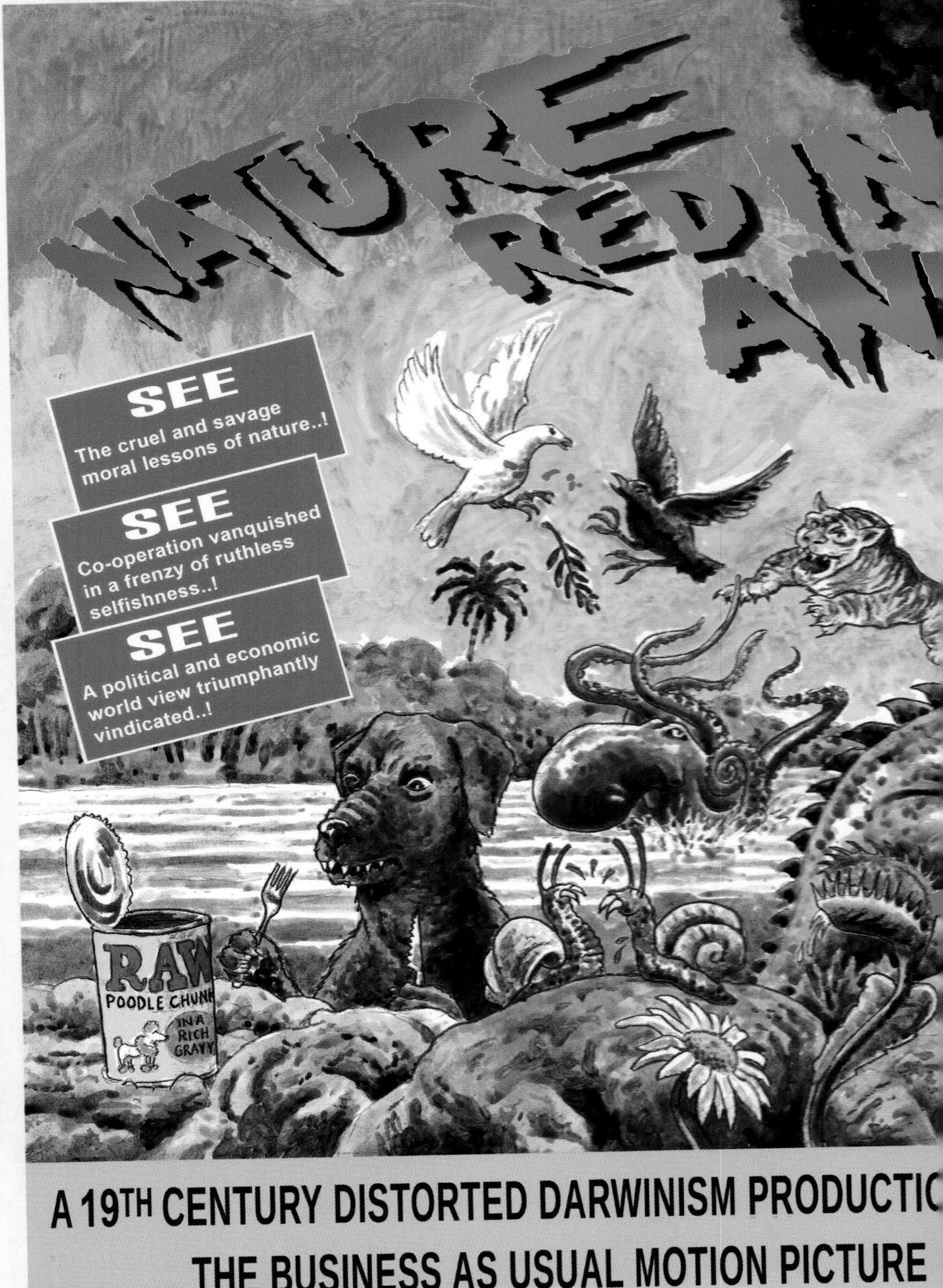
NATURE
SEE
The cruel and savage moral lessons of nature..!
SEE
Co-operation vanquished in a frenzy of ruthless selfishness..!
SEE
A political and economic world view triumphantly vindicated..!
RAW
POODLE CHUNK
IN A RICH GRAVY
A 19TH CENTURY DISTORTED DARWINISM PRODUCTIO
THE BUSINESS AS USUAL MOTION PICTURE

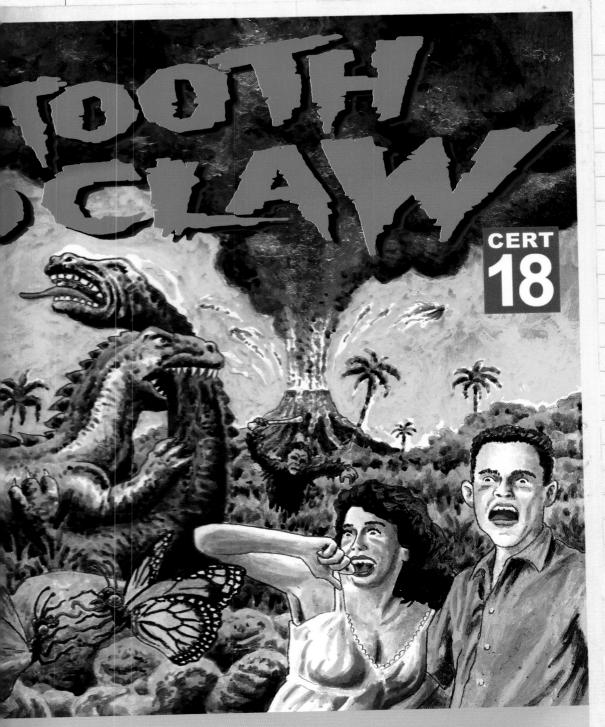

TOOTH CLAW

ASSOCIATION WITH

PANY

STARRING **THE SELFISH GENE**

SCREENPLAY BY **ALFRED, LORD TENNYSON**

From the smallest to the largest scale, between both members of the same species and unrelated ones, co-operation is everywhere.

REVOLVING AND EVOLVING

Volvox is a microscopic, spherical alga found all over the world in freshwater ponds and even in puddles. On closer examination, the organism is revealed to be a colony of thousands of smaller cells, all working together.

Each individual part of the organism has its own 'flagella' tails, and an 'eye' spot.

The colony has a front and back end - individuals at the front have stronger eye spots, those at the rear stronger swimming 'tails'. The colony swims through water by the co-ordinated movements of all of its members.

SO WE'RE NOW TOO BIG TO FAIL, RIGHT..?

NAH. WE'RE JUST TOO BIG TO EAT.

It's likely that Volvox evolved the strategy of clustering together in colonies simply in order to be too big to eat.

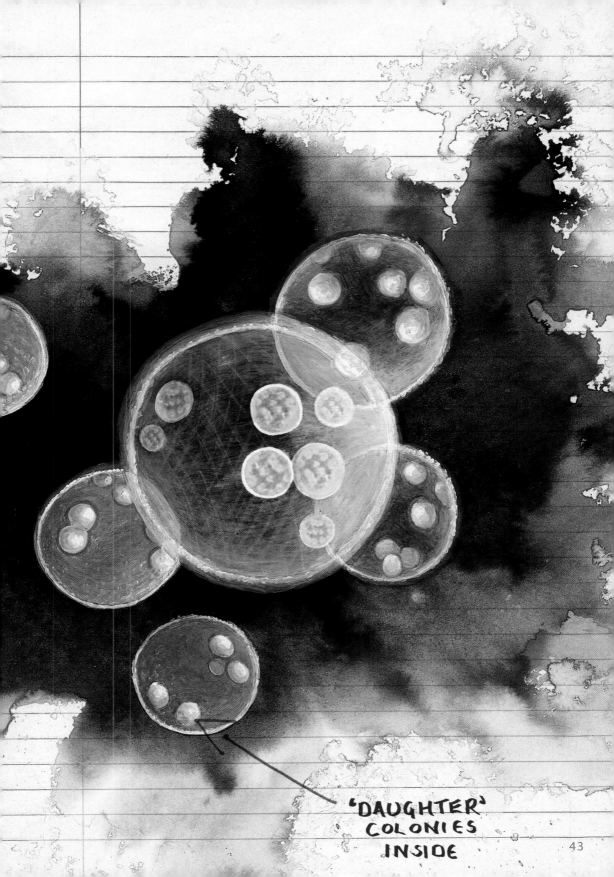

'DAUGHTER'
COLONIES
INSIDE

43

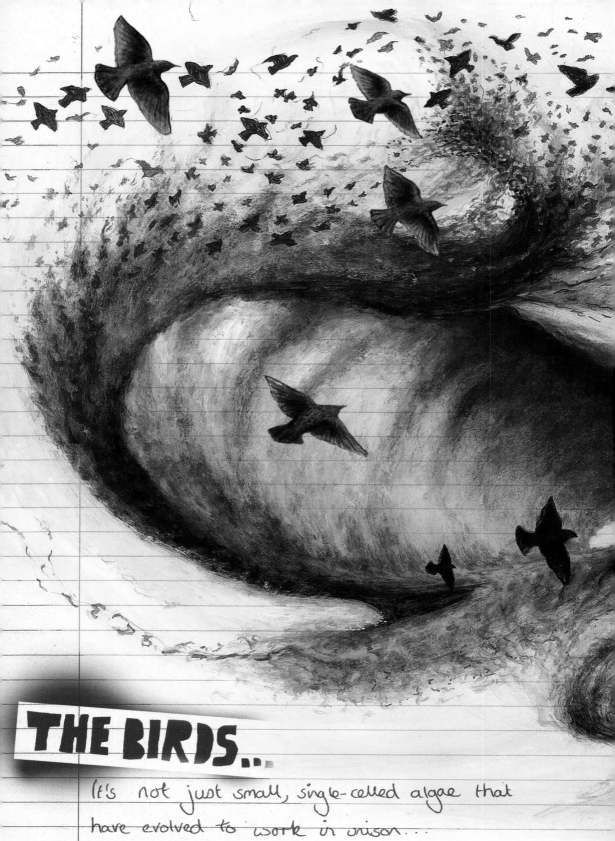

THE BIRDS...

It's not just small, single-celled algae that have evolved to work in unison...

Many creatures swarm together as a survival or efficiency strategy. It's thought that schools of fish and flocks of birds use this group behaviour to startle and confuse predators by the dramatic and shimmering twists and turns they execute, preventing the hunting animal from 'locking on' to any given target.

One of the most visually spectacular and fluid displays of such co-ordinated collective behaviour occurs when swarms of up to one hundred thousand Starlings twist and turn in the air before settling down to their communal roosts.

This is known as a 'murmuration'. The huge and astonishing aerial display is often described as resembling a single giant organism undulating through the sky.

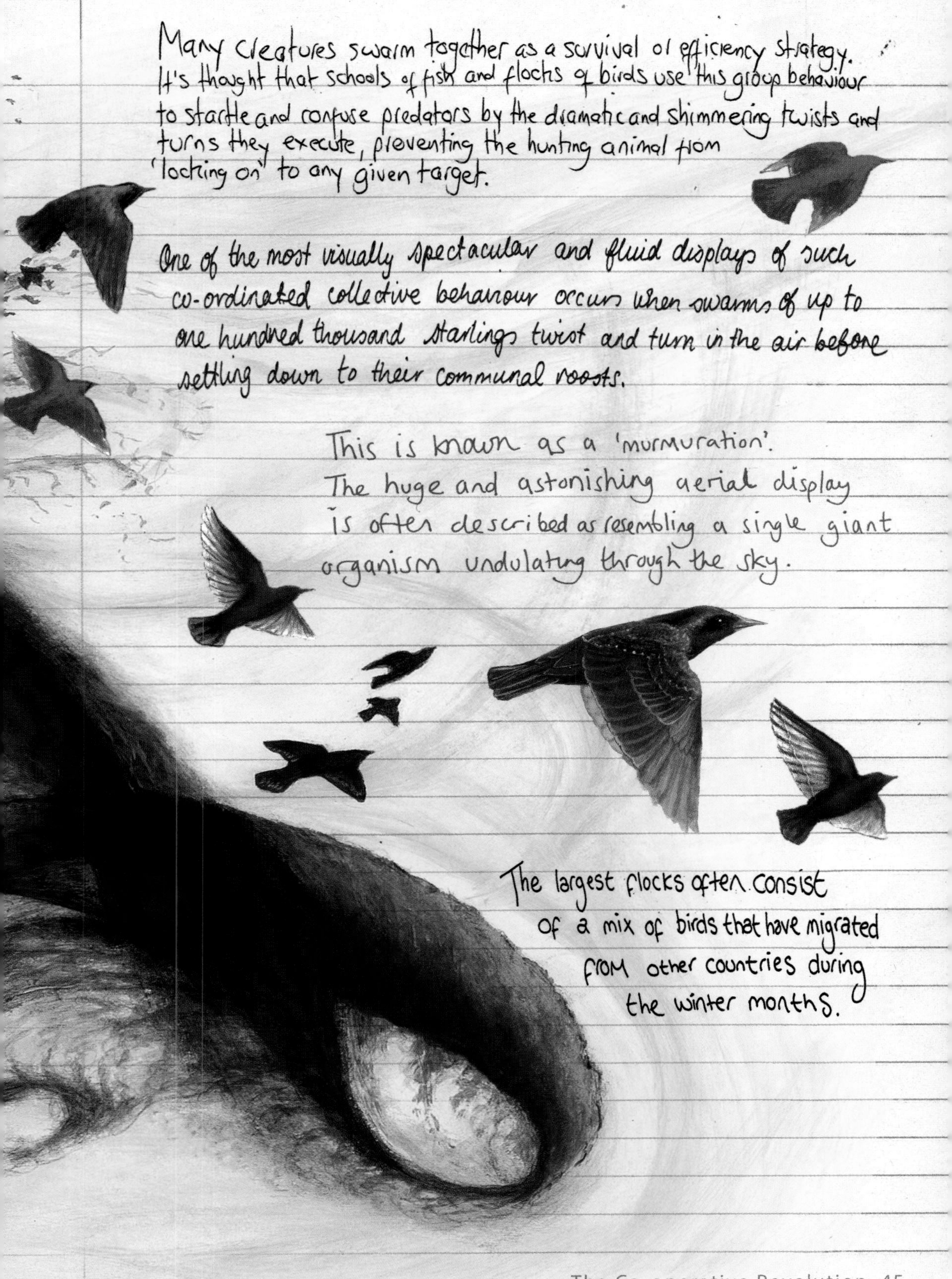

The largest flocks often consist of a mix of birds that have migrated from other countries during the winter months.

> "What does not benefit the hive is no benefit to the bee."
> **Marcus Aurelius**

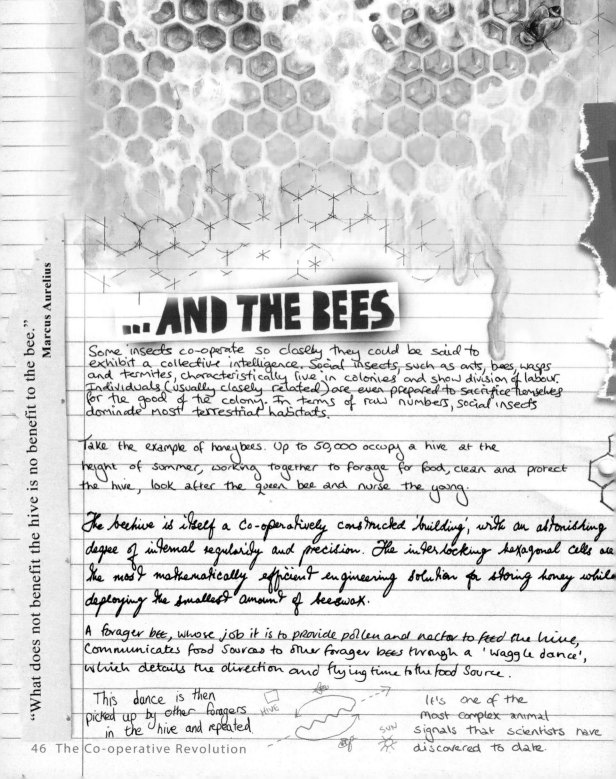

... AND THE BEES

Some insects co-operate so closely they could be said to exhibit a collective intelligence. Social insects, such as ants, bees, wasps and termites, characteristically live in colonies and show division of labour. Individuals (usually closely related) are even prepared to sacrifice themselves for the good of the colony. In terms of raw numbers, social insects dominate most terrestrial habitats.

Take the example of honeybees. Up to 50,000 occupy a hive at the height of summer, working together to forage for food, clean and protect the hive, look after the queen bee and nurse the young.

The beehive is itself a co-operatively constructed 'building', with an astonishing degree of internal regularity and precision. The interlocking hexagonal cells are the most mathematically efficient engineering solution for storing honey while deploying the smallest amount of beeswax.

A forager bee, whose job it is to provide pollen and nectar to feed the hive, communicates food sources to other forager bees through a 'waggle dance', which details the direction and flying time to the food source.

This dance is then picked up by other foragers in the hive and repeated

HIVE
SUN

It's one of the most complex animal signals that scientists have discovered to date.

It's recently been discovered that some bees specialize as 'heater bees', and raise the temperature of specific sections of the hive.

They vibrate their abdomens and wing muscles in order to encourage temperature-sensitive larvae to grow into bees with a particular function.

HISTORY & MEMORY
CO-OPERATIVE SOCIETY LIMITED

Beehives have frequently been used by co-operatives as a symbol of collective effort, since a lone honeybee cannot survive on its own but, with others in a beehive, it thrives.

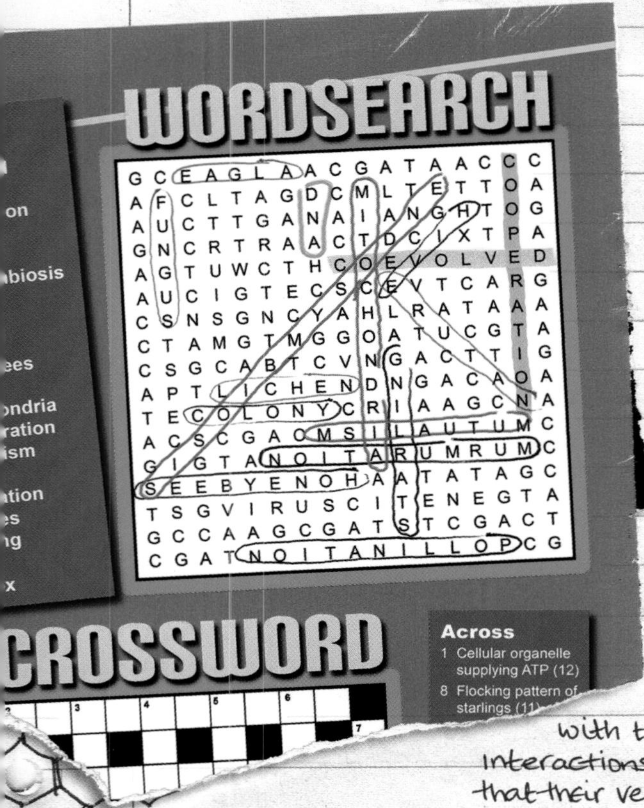

WORDSEARCH

```
G C E A G L A A C G A T A A C C
A F C L T A G D C M L T E T T O
A U C T T G A N A I A N G H T A
G N C R T R A C S T D C I X T P
A G T U W C T H O E V O L V E D
A C I G T E C S C E V T C A R G
C S N S G N C Y A H L R A T A A
C T A M G T M G G O A T U C G T
C S G C A B T C V N G A C T T I
A P T L I C H E N D N G A C A N
T E C O L O N Y C R I A A G C N
A C S C G A O M S I L I A U T U M C
G I G T A N O I T A R U M R U M C
S E E B Y E N O H A A T A T A G C
T S G V I R U S C I T E N E G T A
G C C A A G C G A T S T C G A C T
C G A T N O I T A N I L L O P C G
```

CROSSWORD

Across
1 Cellular organelle supplying ATP (12)
8 Flocking pattern of starlings (11)

on
biosis
ees
ondria
ration
ism
ation
es
g
x

CO-EVOLVED

Co-operative behaviour isn't just confined to members of the same species or a family of closely related individuals. Over millions of years, bees, butterflies, wasps and flies have co-evolved mutually beneficial relationships with tens of thousands of different plants - interactions which are so entwined in some instances that their very survival is connected.

The pollination of flowering plants is a classical example of this. While collecting food such as pollen or nectar, insects unconsciously transfer pollen from the male to the female parts. This facilitates fertilization and ultimately the production of fruits, nuts and seeds. In order to attract and reward pollinators, plants have evolved colourful petals, nutritious nectar and sticky pollen.

Humans depend on this interaction as well. Around one-third of the food we eat is pollinated by honeybees alone, from peanuts, soya beans, onions, carrots, broccoli and sunflowers to apples, oranges, blueberries, cranberries, strawberries, melons, avocados and peaches.

In all, some ninety commercial crops worldwide are kept on the menu by bees and co-operation.

SLOW BUT SURE

Before the microscope, scientists understood lichen to be a simple, single organism. But they then discovered that these humble circles of colour are the product of an intimate symbiotic co-operation between radically different forms of life, typically an alga and a fungus.

The alga photosynthesizes to produce fuel for itself and the fungus, while the fungus provides a foothold and shelter, as well as access to inorganic nutrients.

Lichen may grow at less than a millimetre a year, but they are astonishingly long-lived - some are older than the pyramids of Egypt.

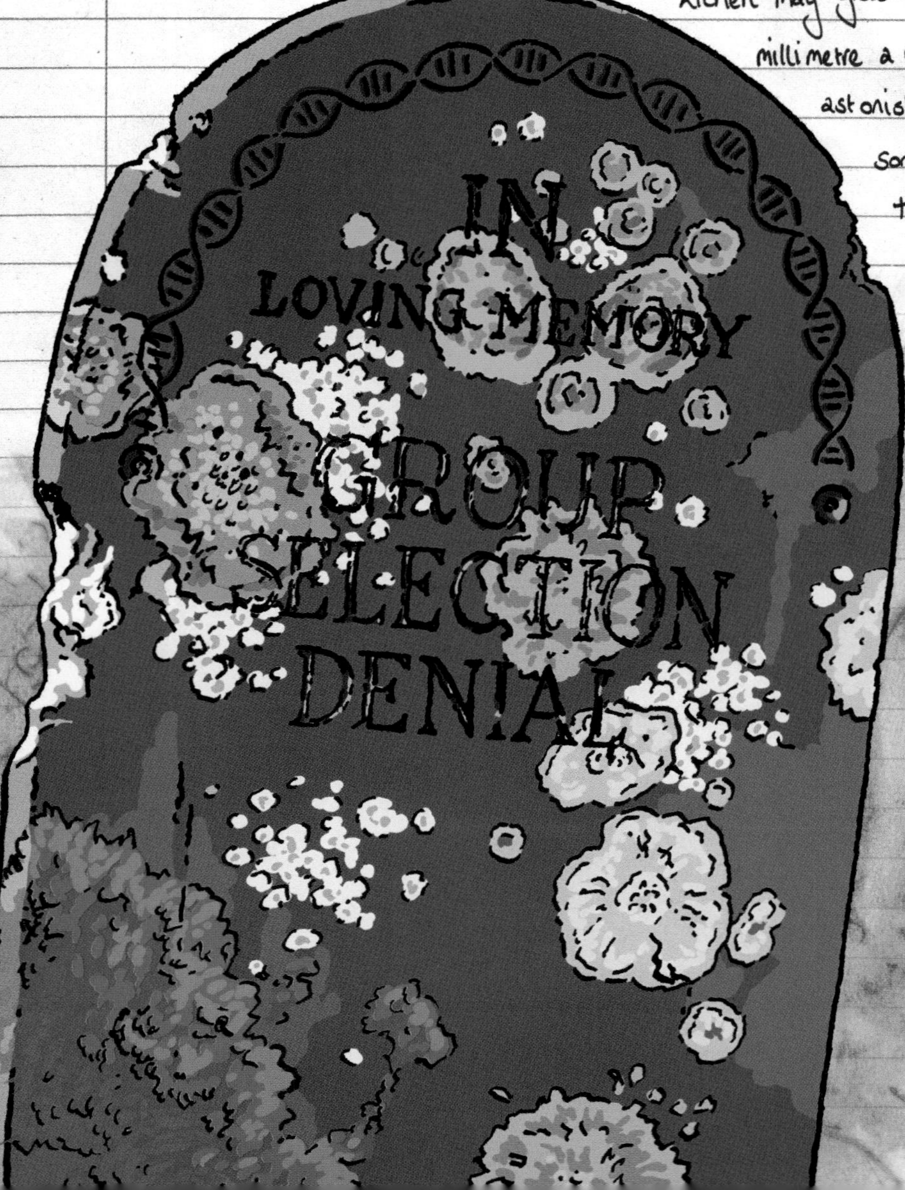
IN LOVING MEMORY
GROUP SELECTION DENIAL

BACK TO OUR ROOTS

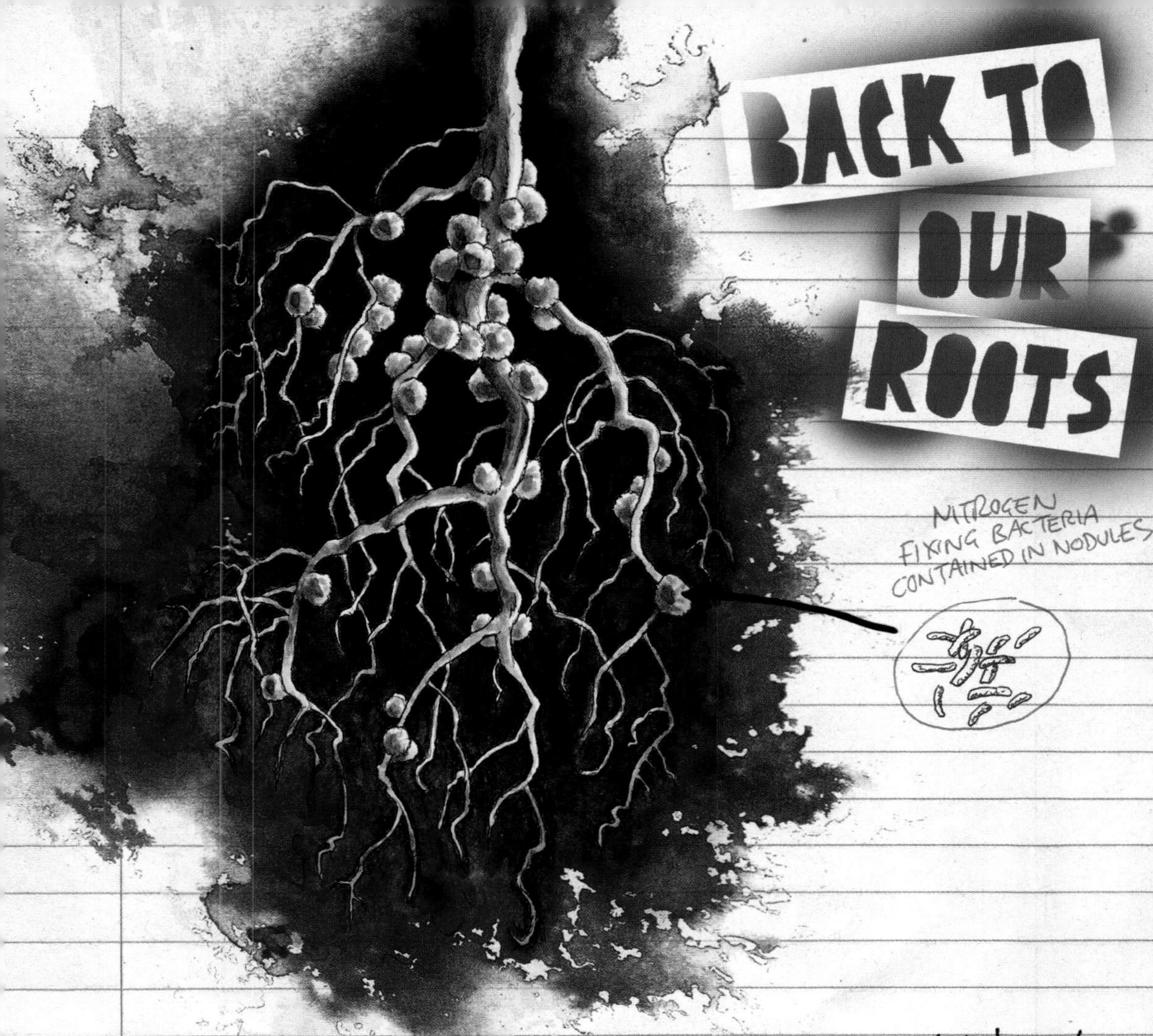
NITROGEN FIXING BACTERIA CONTAINED IN NODULES

Nitrogen is one of the essential elements of life, but it needs to be 'fixed' and made accessible in order that it can be utilized in DNA and proteins. Many plants encourage specific nitrogen fixing bacteria to colonize their roots and take residence in purpose built swellings, or nodules.

The bacteria get a safe haven, and the plant the by-product nutrients it needs to grow. These symbiotic relationships are vital not just to the plants and bacteria involved, but to the fertility of the entire soil ecosystem.

That's why, for hundreds of years, farmers have used legumes such as clover and beans as break crops to boost soil fertility.

Humans have now discovered how to produce fertilizer on an industrial scale, although our processes are a little cruder, requiring searing temperatures of 500°C and atmospheric pressures some 200 times greater than those these humble plants and bacteria operate in.

A STING IN THE TALE

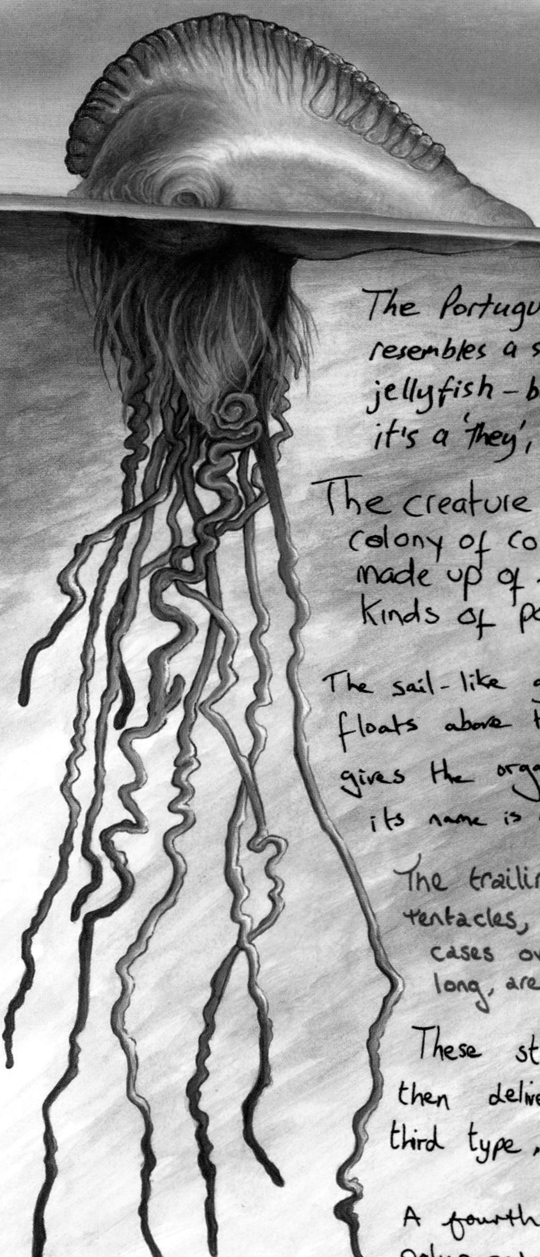

The Portuguese man'o war resembles a straightforward jellyfish – but, in reality, it's a 'they', not an 'it'.

The creature is actually a colony of colonies, and is made up of four different kinds of polyps.

The sail-like gasbag that floats above the water and gives the organism its name is one.

The trailing poisonous tentacles, in some cases over 10 metres long, are another.

These sting prey and then deliver it to a third type, the stomach.

A fourth kind of polyp acts as the reproductive organs.

LAYERS WITHIN LAYERS

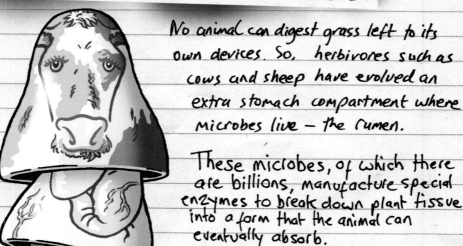

No animal can digest grass left to its own devices. So, herbivores such as cows and sheep have evolved an extra stomach compartment where microbes live — the rumen.

These microbes, of which there are billions, manufacture special enzymes to break down plant tissue into a form that the animal can eventually absorb.

The microbial community within the rumen is incredibly complex — and is very much an ecosystem in its own right.

Bacteria will typically reside on the outside of a protozoan, helping it to process the complex chemical soup it lives within.

The majority of feeding relationships between plants and herbivores and their parasites are probably mediated by these complex symbiotic groups, accounting for over half the species on Earth.

LIFE IS MADE OF CO-OPERATION

But perhaps the most startling co-operative relationships of all lie deep within our cells. Amazingly, it transpires that the mitochondria that power animal cells (and the chloroplasts that power plant cells) are derived from bacteria that took up residence there hundreds of millions of years ago.

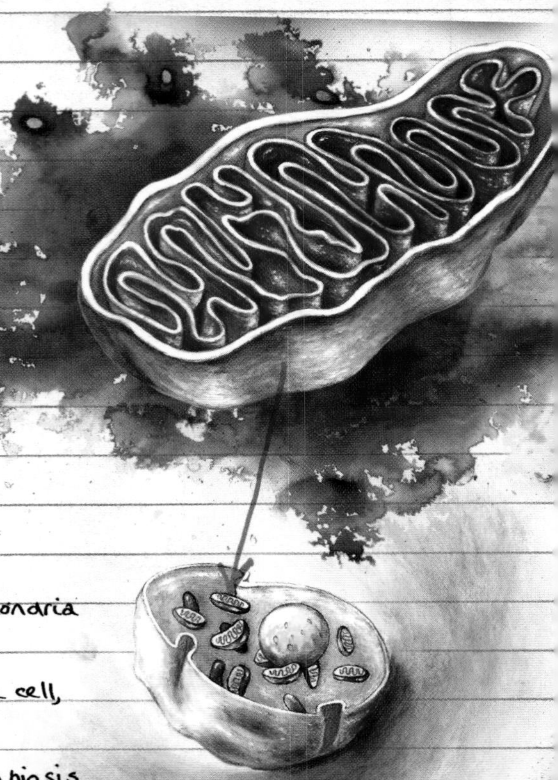

The curious similarity between bacteria and these cellular organelles was first noted more than a century ago. However, despite the compelling evidence that both mitochondria and chloroplasts have their own DNA and reproduce independently from the rest of the cell, it required the dogged persistence of Lynn Margulis and her theory of endosymbiosis before mainstream science listened.

But then the implications were enormous – namely, that the creation of new forms of life through permanent symbiotic agreements is the principal avenue of evolution for all higher organisms.

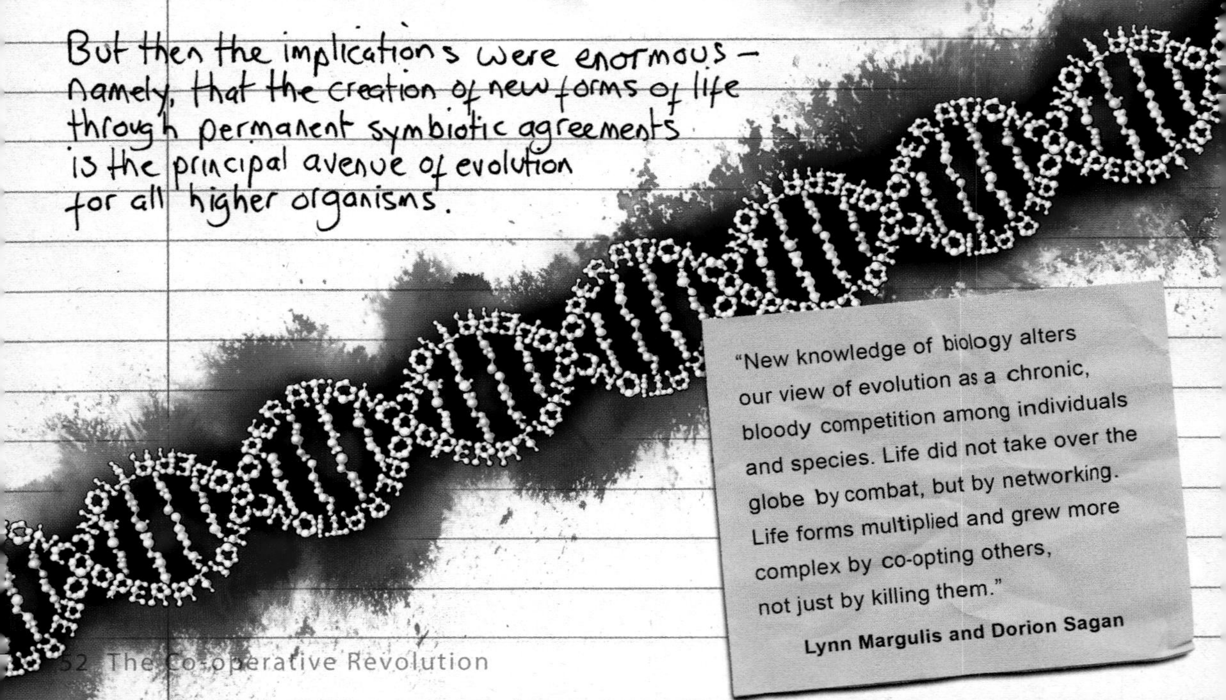

"New knowledge of biology alters our view of evolution as a chronic, bloody competition among individuals and species. Life did not take over the globe by combat, but by networking. Life forms multiplied and grew more complex by co-opting others, not just by killing them."

Lynn Margulis and Dorion Sagan

GOOD GUYS CAN FINISH FIRST

For decades we have been taught that our cells are full of 'selfish genes', each seeking to thrust itself into the next generation – and that this alone is the raw material of natural selection.

However, while the selfish gene is very real, there are bigger and more optimistic truths out there in nature – and within our own bodies. According to multi-level selection theory, life is a nested hierarchy of units: genes within individuals, individuals within groups, groups within a population and even clusters of groups – and co-operation can be advantageous at every level.

SURVIVAL OF THE FITTEST GROUPS IS AS FEASIBLE AS SURVIVAL OF THE FITTEST INDIVIDUALS AND THIS FORCE HAS PLAYED A CRUCIAL ROLE IN SHAPING BOTH OUR GENES AND OUR CULTURE

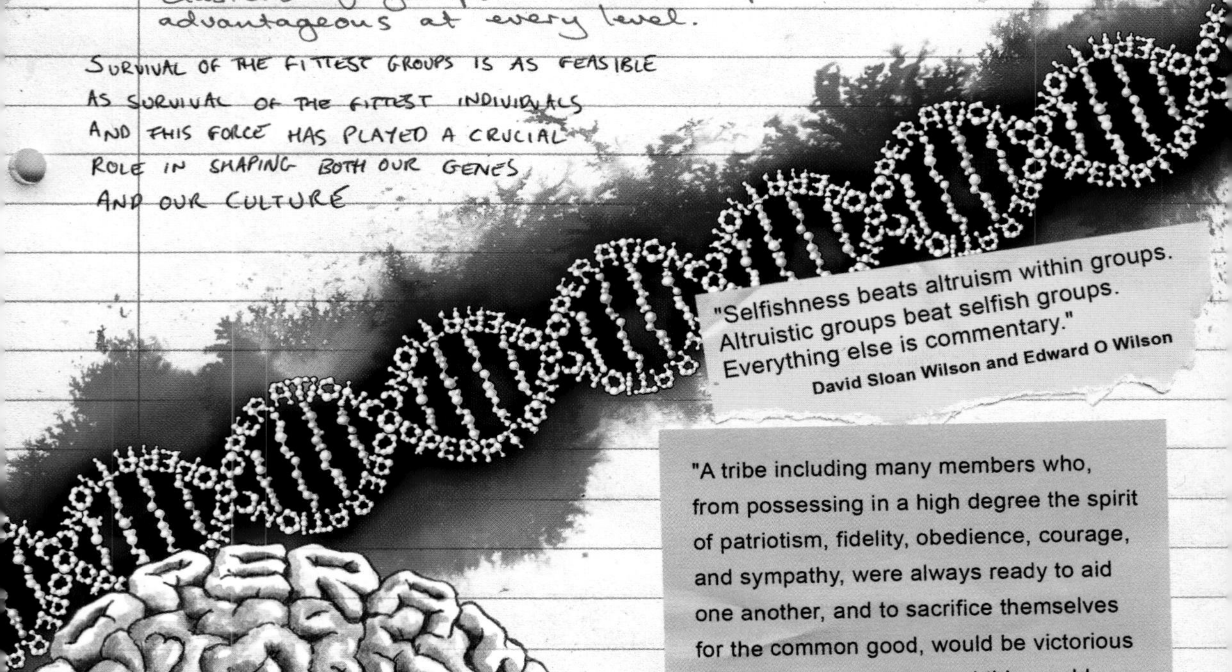

"Selfishness beats altruism within groups. Altruistic groups beat selfish groups. Everything else is commentary."

David Sloan Wilson and Edward O Wilson

"A tribe including many members who, from possessing in a high degree the spirit of patriotism, fidelity, obedience, courage, and sympathy, were always ready to aid one another, and to sacrifice themselves for the common good, would be victorious over most other tribes; and this would be natural selection."

Charles Darwin

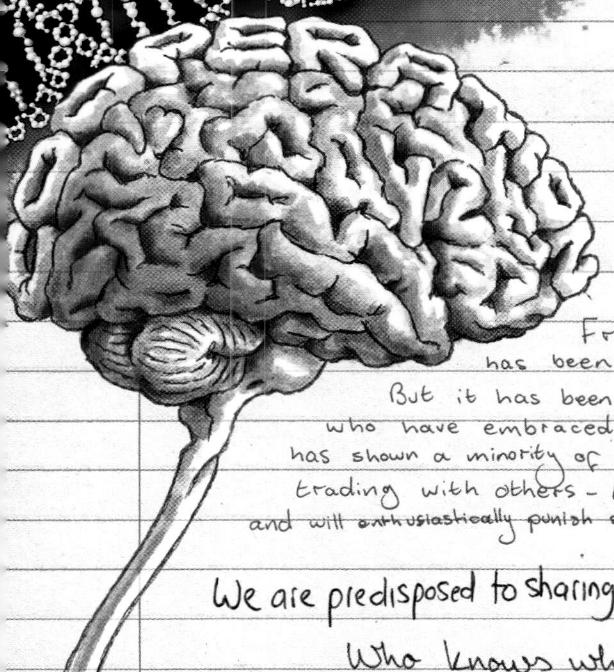

From amoebas to zebras, co-operation has been a major evolutionary force shaping life. But it has been humans, more than any other species who have embraced it to greatest effect. Study after study has shown a minority of people are amoral and self-regarding when trading with others – the majority prefer to strike a fair deal and will enthusiastically punish shirkers who exploit the co-operation of others.

We are predisposed to sharing and trusting, and are much the better for it.

Who knows what the next steps might be...

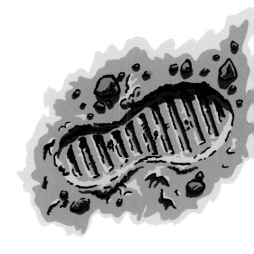

Tomorrow

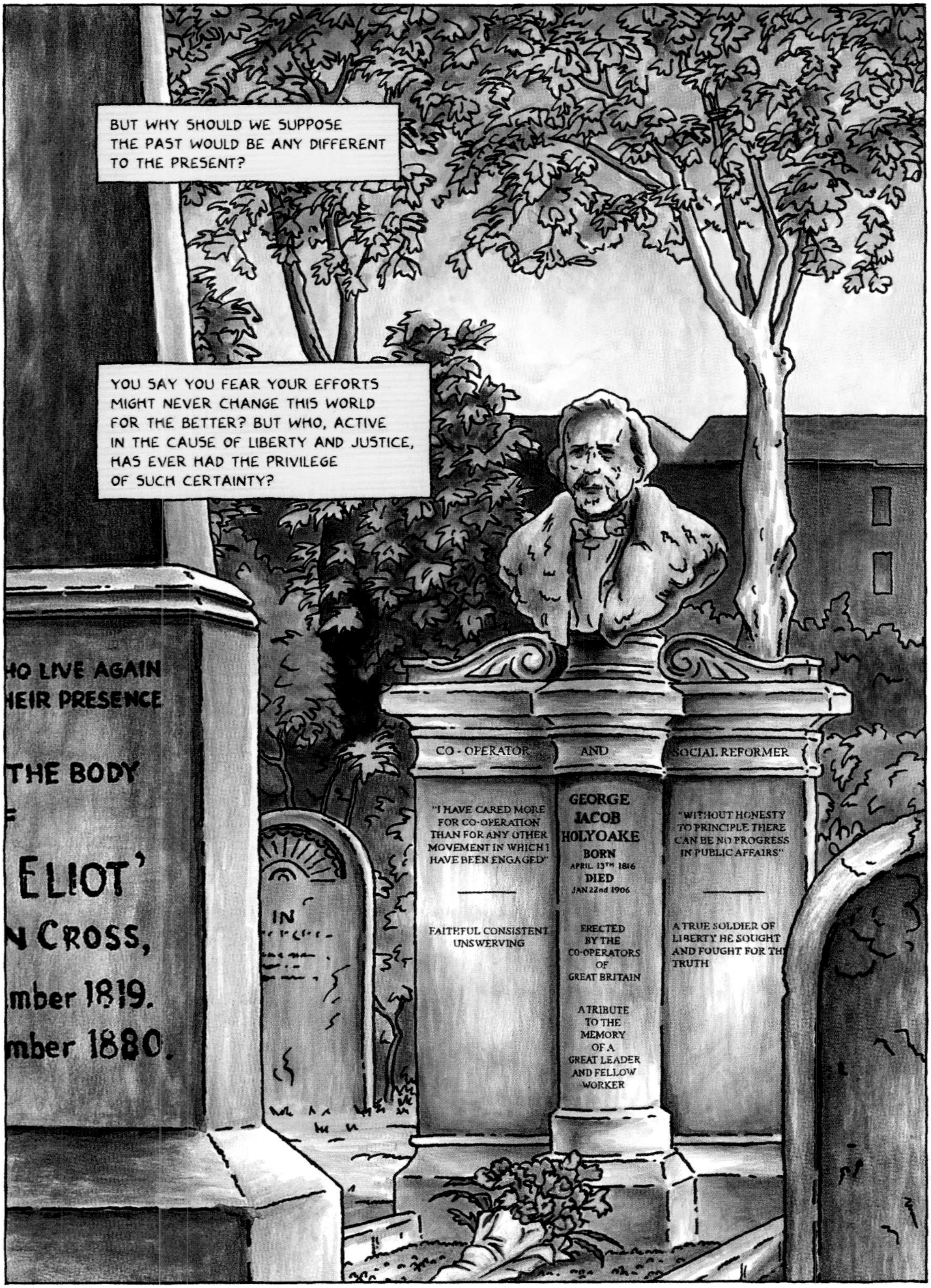
BUT WHY SHOULD WE SUPPOSE THE PAST WOULD BE ANY DIFFERENT TO THE PRESENT?
YOU SAY YOU FEAR YOUR EFFORTS MIGHT NEVER CHANGE THIS WORLD FOR THE BETTER? BUT WHO, ACTIVE IN THE CAUSE OF LIBERTY AND JUSTICE, HAS EVER HAD THE PRIVILEGE OF SUCH CERTAINTY?
HO LIVE AGAIN
HEIR PRESENCE
THE BODY
ELIOT'
N CROSS,
mber 1819.
mber 1880.
CO-OPERATOR
AND
SOCIAL REFORMER
"I HAVE CARED MORE FOR CO-OPERATION THAN FOR ANY OTHER MOVEMENT IN WHICH I HAVE BEEN ENGAGED"
FAITHFUL CONSISTENT UNSWERVING
GEORGE JACOB HOLYOAKE
BORN
APRIL 13TH 1816
DIED
JAN 22nd 1906
ERECTED BY THE CO-OPERATORS OF GREAT BRITAIN
A TRIBUTE TO THE MEMORY OF A GREAT LEADER AND FELLOW WORKER
"WITHOUT HONESTY TO PRINCIPLE THERE CAN BE NO PROGRESS IN PUBLIC AFFAIRS"
A TRUE SOLDIER OF LIBERTY HE SOUGHT AND FOUGHT FOR THE TRUTH
IN

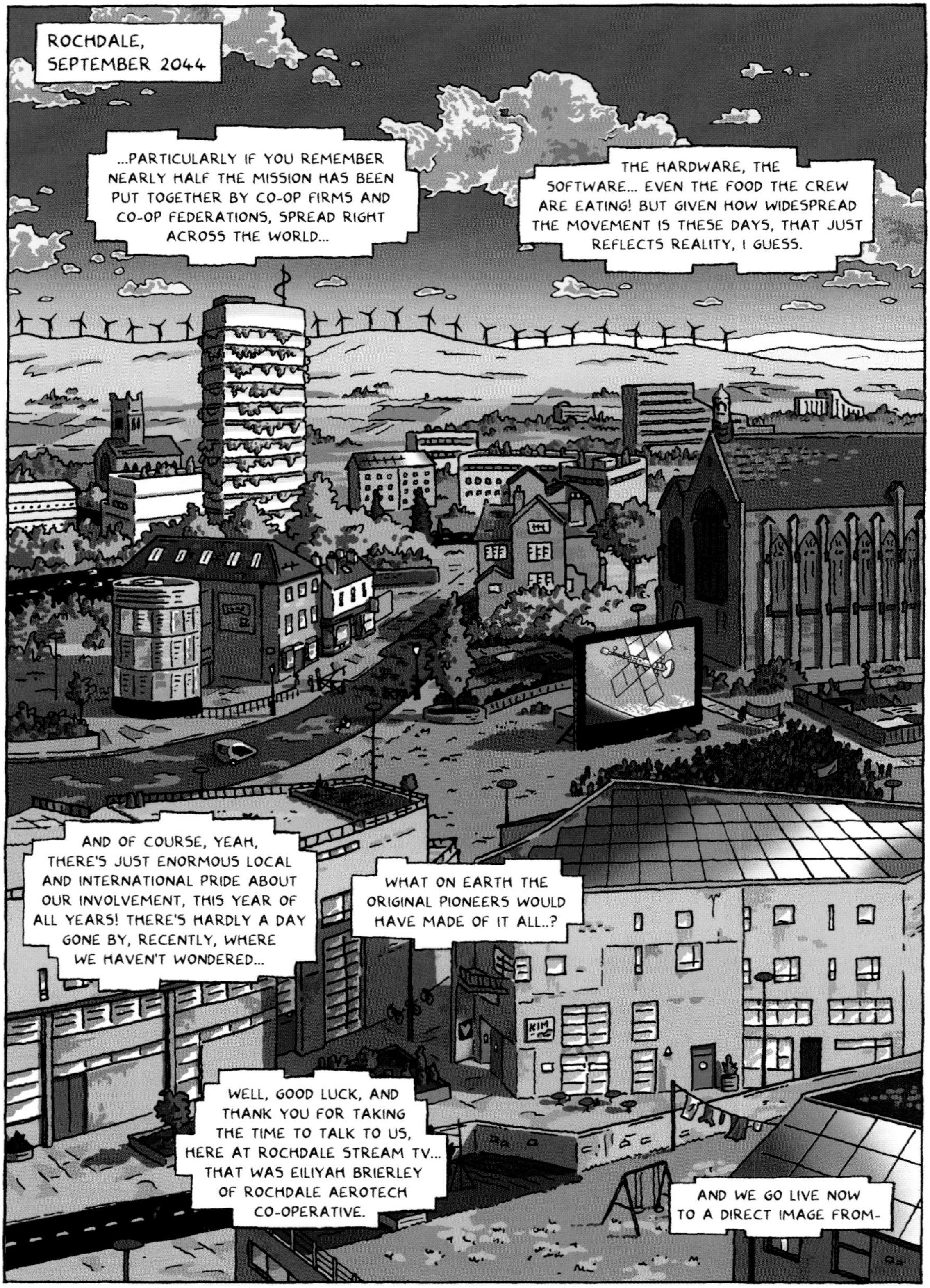
ROCHDALE, SEPTEMBER 2044
...PARTICULARLY IF YOU REMEMBER NEARLY HALF THE MISSION HAS BEEN PUT TOGETHER BY CO-OP FIRMS AND CO-OP FEDERATIONS, SPREAD RIGHT ACROSS THE WORLD...
THE HARDWARE, THE SOFTWARE... EVEN THE FOOD THE CREW ARE EATING! BUT GIVEN HOW WIDESPREAD THE MOVEMENT IS THESE DAYS, THAT JUST REFLECTS REALITY, I GUESS.
AND OF COURSE, YEAH, THERE'S JUST ENORMOUS LOCAL AND INTERNATIONAL PRIDE ABOUT OUR INVOLVEMENT, THIS YEAR OF ALL YEARS! THERE'S HARDLY A DAY GONE BY, RECENTLY, WHERE WE HAVEN'T WONDERED...
WHAT ON EARTH THE ORIGINAL PIONEERS WOULD HAVE MADE OF IT ALL..?
WELL, GOOD LUCK, AND THANK YOU FOR TAKING THE TIME TO TALK TO US, HERE AT ROCHDALE STREAM TV... THAT WAS EILIYAH BRIERLEY OF ROCHDALE AEROTECH CO-OPERATIVE.
AND WE GO LIVE NOW TO A DIRECT IMAGE FROM-
KIM

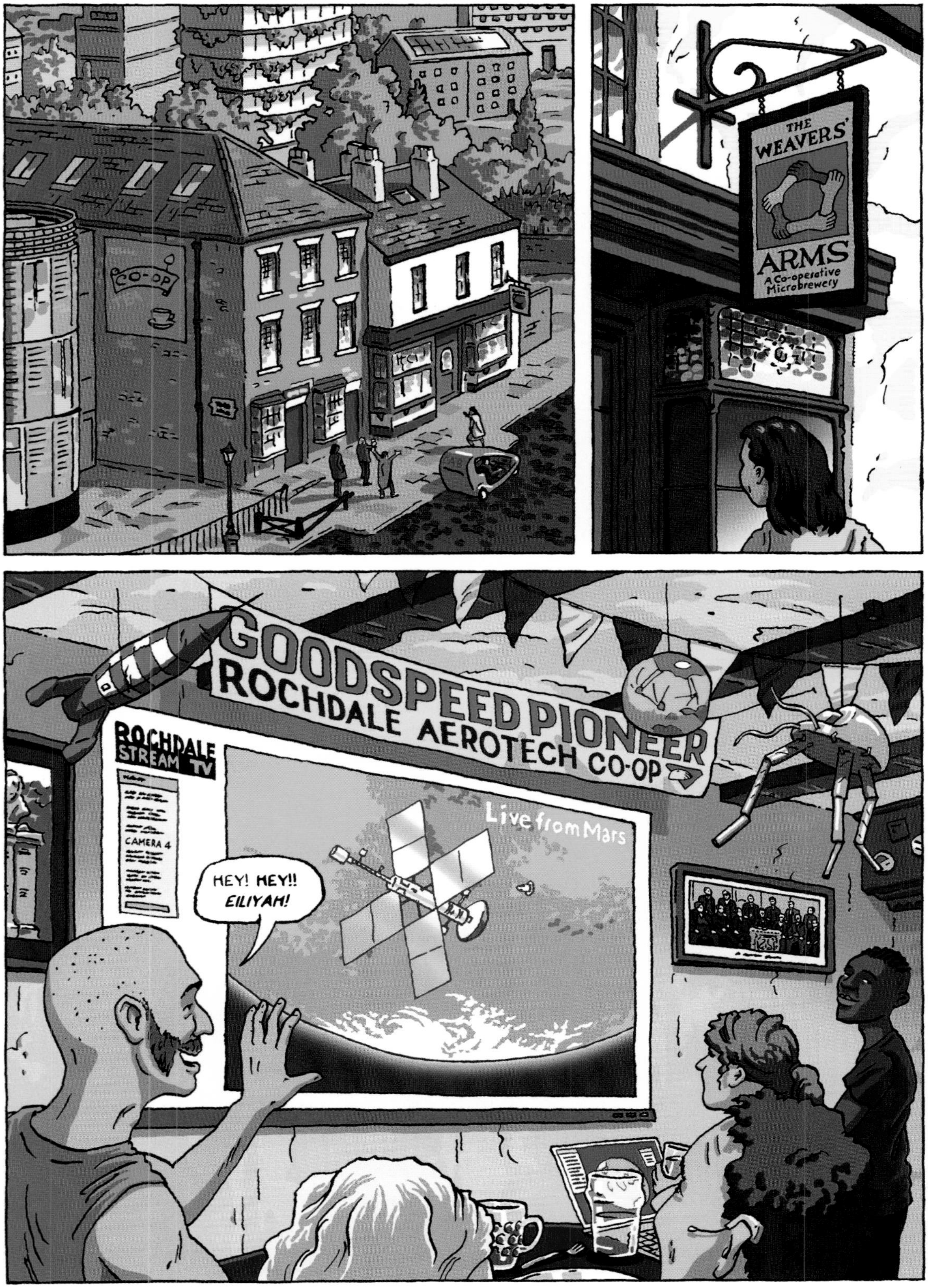
CO-OP
THE WEAVERS' ARMS
A Co-operative Microbrewery
GOODSPEED PIONEER
ROCHDALE AEROTECH CO-OP
ROCHDALE STREAM TV
CAMERA 4
Live from Mars
HEY! HEY!! EILIYAH!

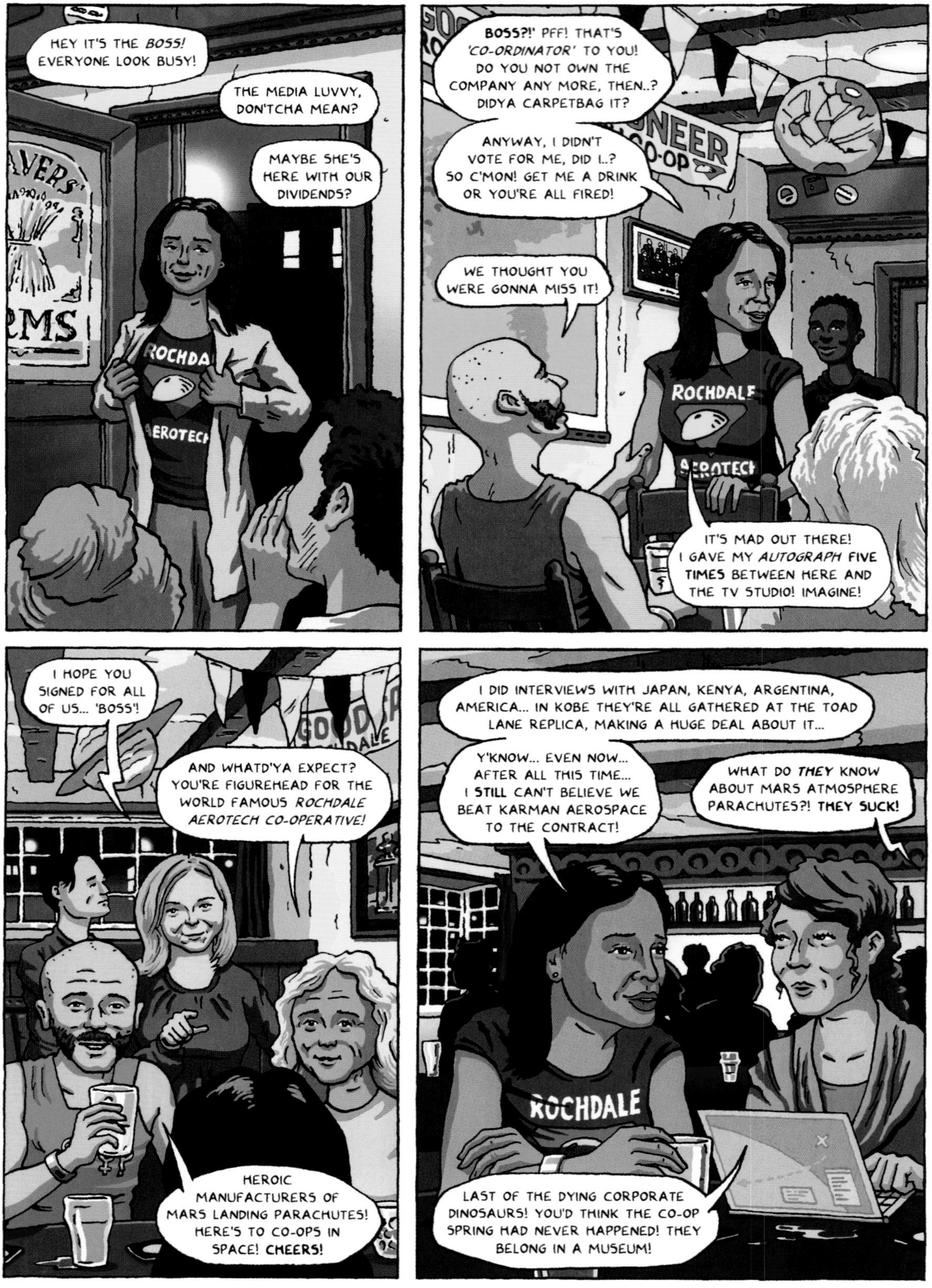
HEY IT'S THE *BOSS!* EVERYONE LOOK BUSY!
THE MEDIA LUVVY, DON'TCHA MEAN?
MAYBE SHE'S HERE WITH OUR DIVIDENDS?
BOSS?!' PFF! THAT'S *'CO-ORDINATOR'* TO YOU! DO YOU NOT OWN THE COMPANY ANY MORE, THEN..? DIDYA CARPETBAG IT?
ANYWAY, I DIDN'T VOTE FOR ME, DID I..? SO C'MON! GET ME A DRINK OR YOU'RE ALL FIRED!
WE THOUGHT YOU WERE GONNA MISS IT!
ROCHDALE
IT'S MAD OUT THERE! I GAVE MY *AUTOGRAPH* **FIVE TIMES** BETWEEN HERE AND THE TV STUDIO! IMAGINE!
I HOPE YOU SIGNED FOR ALL OF US... 'BOSS'!
AND WHATD'YA EXPECT? YOU'RE FIGUREHEAD FOR THE WORLD FAMOUS *ROCHDALE AEROTECH CO-OPERATIVE!*
HEROIC MANUFACTURERS OF MARS LANDING PARACHUTES! HERE'S TO CO-OPS IN SPACE! **CHEERS!**
I DID INTERVIEWS WITH JAPAN, KENYA, ARGENTINA, AMERICA... IN KOBE THEY'RE ALL GATHERED AT THE TOAD LANE REPLICA, MAKING A HUGE DEAL ABOUT IT...
Y'KNOW... EVEN NOW... AFTER ALL THIS TIME... I **STILL** CAN'T BELIEVE WE BEAT KARMAN AEROSPACE TO THE CONTRACT!
WHAT DO ***THEY*** KNOW ABOUT MARS ATMOSPHERE PARACHUTES?! **THEY SUCK!**
ROCHDALE
LAST OF THE DYING CORPORATE DINOSAURS! YOU'D THINK THE CO-OP SPRING HAD NEVER HAPPENED! THEY BELONG IN A MUSEUM!

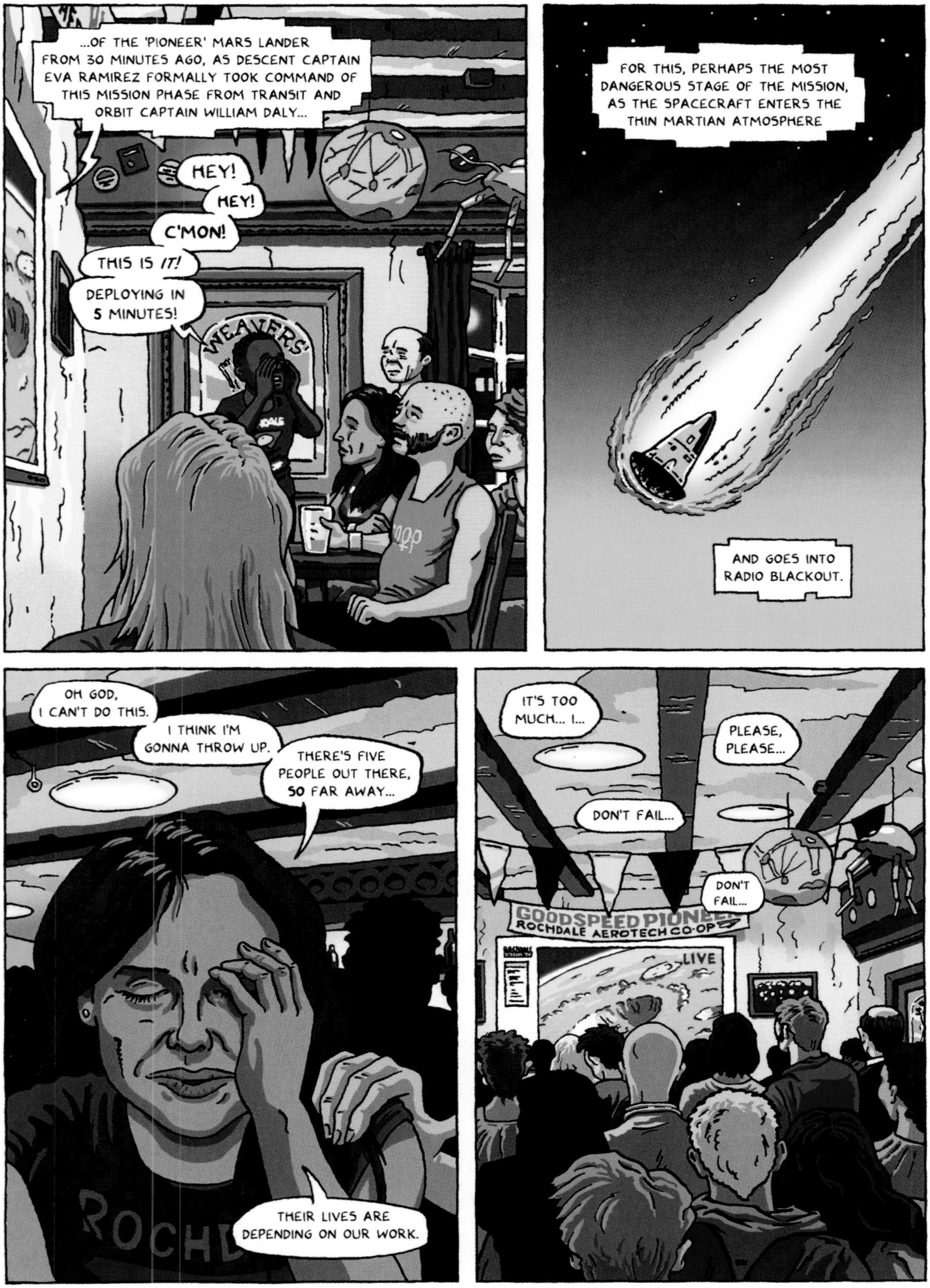
...OF THE 'PIONEER' MARS LANDER FROM 30 MINUTES AGO, AS DESCENT CAPTAIN EVA RAMIREZ FORMALLY TOOK COMMAND OF THIS MISSION PHASE FROM TRANSIT AND ORBIT CAPTAIN WILLIAM DALY...
HEY!
HEY!
C'MON!
THIS IS *IT!*
DEPLOYING IN **5** MINUTES!
WEAVERS'
FOR THIS, PERHAPS THE MOST DANGEROUS STAGE OF THE MISSION, AS THE SPACECRAFT ENTERS THE THIN MARTIAN ATMOSPHERE
AND GOES INTO RADIO BLACKOUT.
OH GOD, I CAN'T DO THIS.
I THINK I'M GONNA THROW UP.
THERE'S FIVE PEOPLE OUT THERE, **SO** FAR AWAY...
THEIR LIVES ARE DEPENDING ON OUR WORK.
IT'S TOO MUCH... I...
PLEASE, PLEASE...
DON'T FAIL...
DON'T FAIL...
ROCHDALE AEROTECH CO-OP
LIVE

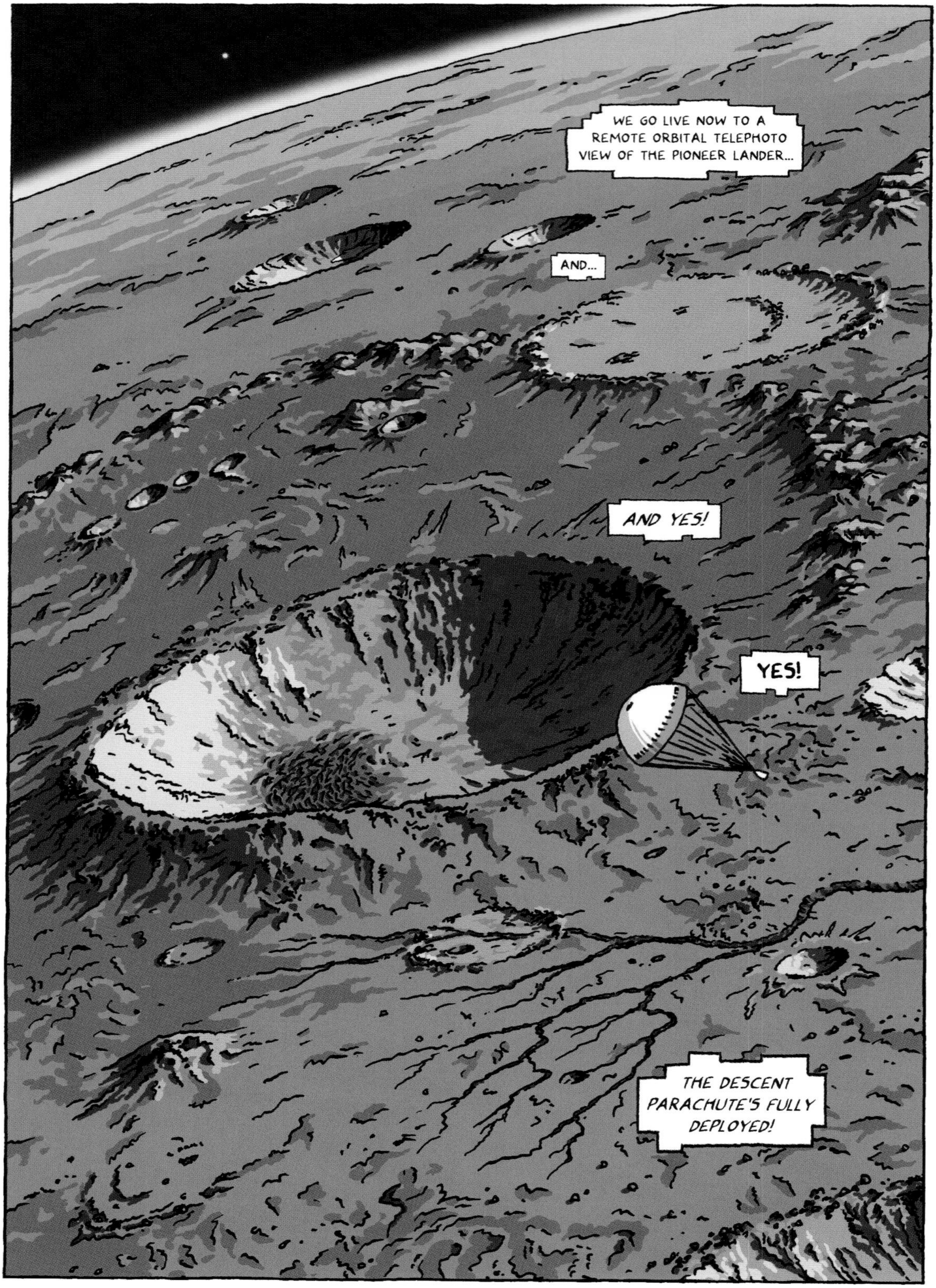
WE GO LIVE NOW TO A REMOTE ORBITAL TELEPHOTO VIEW OF THE PIONEER LANDER...
AND...
AND YES!
YES!
THE DESCENT PARACHUTE'S FULLY DEPLOYED!

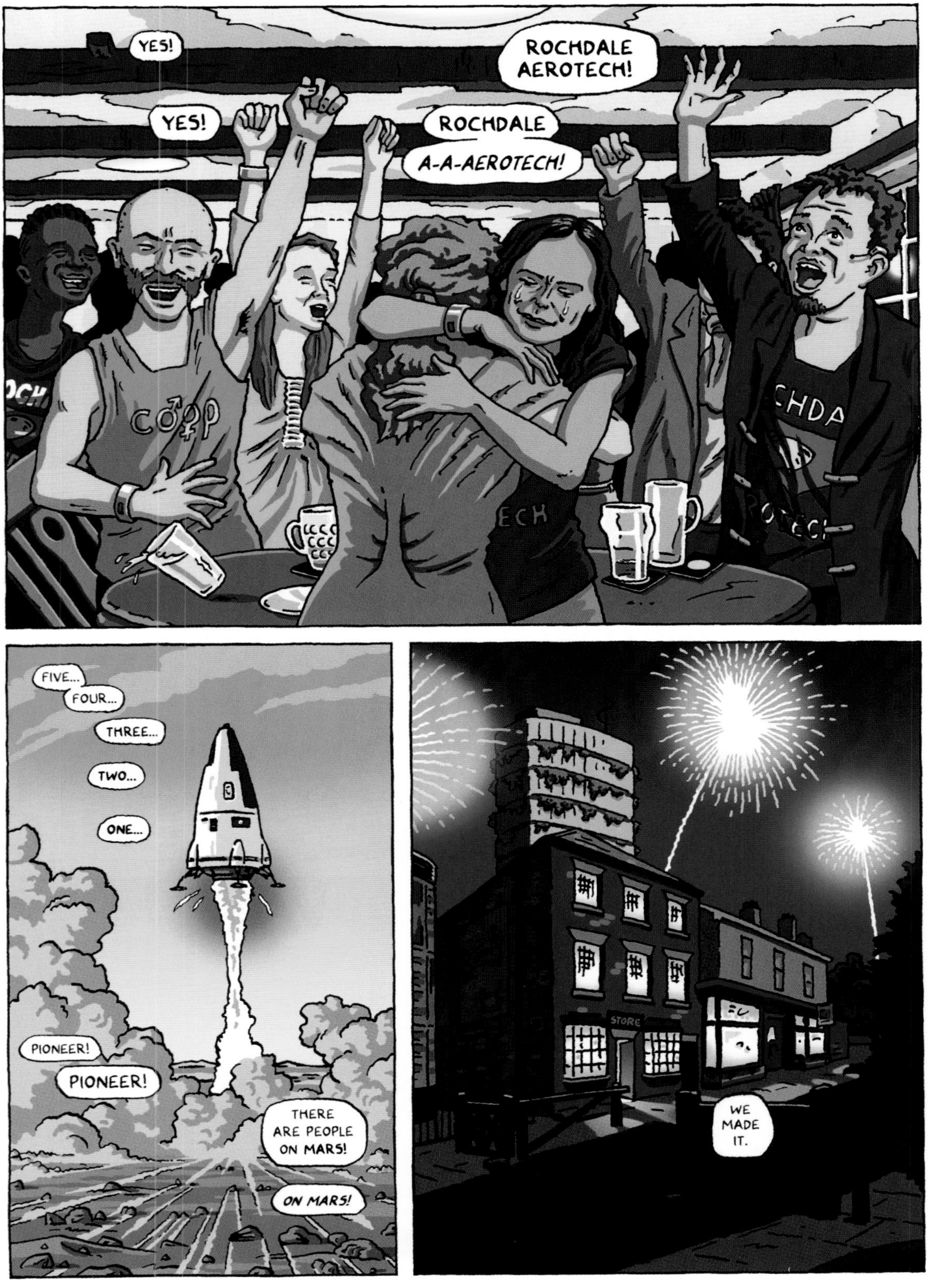
YES!
YES!
ROCHDALE AEROTECH!
ROCHDALE
A-A-AEROTECH!
FIVE...
FOUR...
THREE...
TWO...
ONE...
PIONEER!
PIONEER!
THERE ARE PEOPLE ON MARS!
ON MARS!
STORE
WE MADE IT.

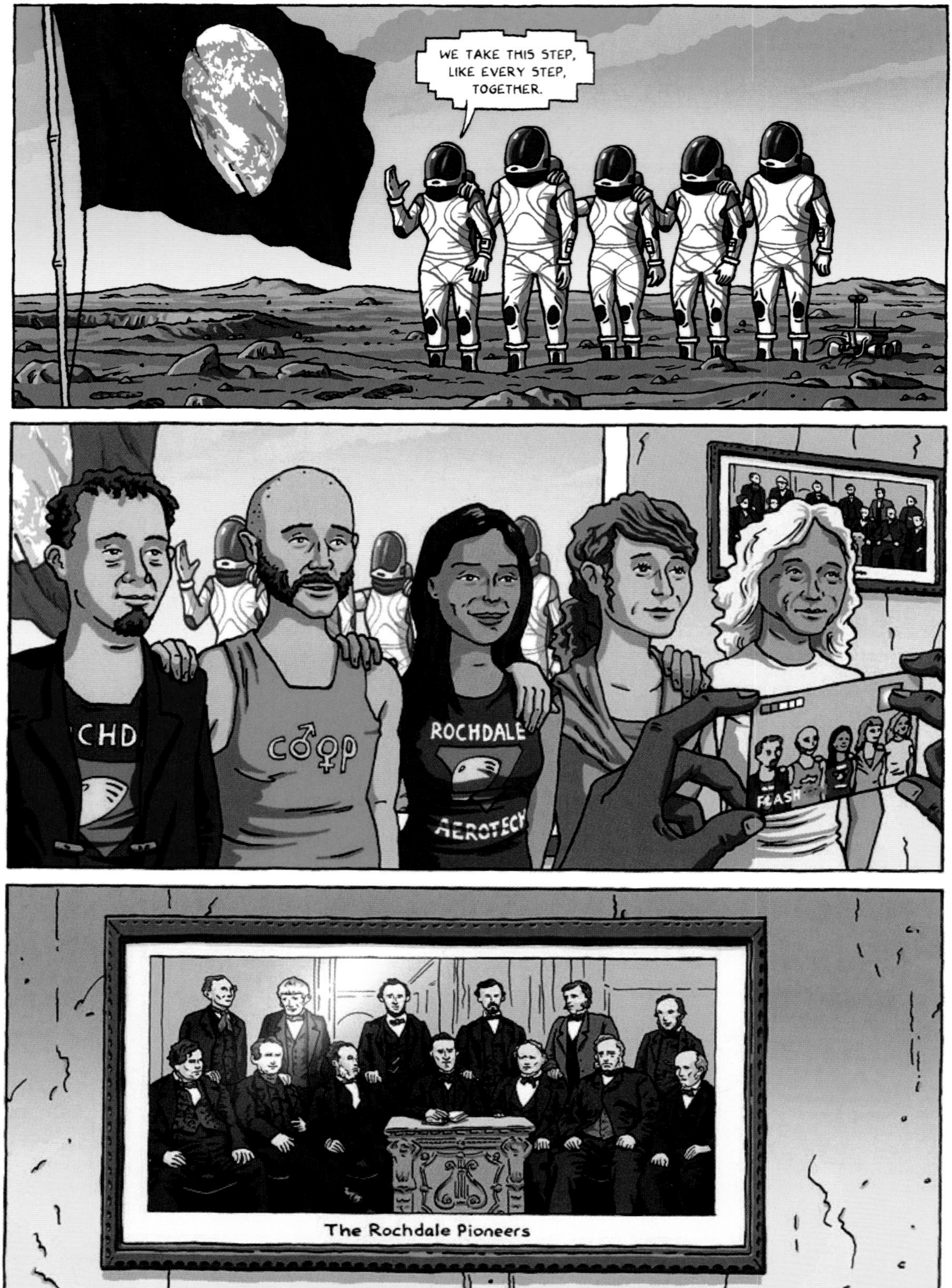
WE TAKE THIS STEP, LIKE EVERY STEP, TOGETHER.
ROCHDALE
AEROTECH
FLASH
The Rochdale Pioneers

Timeline

Co-operation Through History

Key: black = UK co-operative movement events;
blue = international co-operative movement events; red = general UK and international events.

1769
Scotland's Fenwick Weavers' establish an enterprise for the bulk purchasing of food – the earliest co-operative for which there are full records.

Robert Owen.

1799
Robert Owen and partners purchase the New Lanark Twist Company in Scotland. Owen introduces reforms – including good housing and wages, nurseries and education for workers' children, and free healthcare – all while running a profitable mill.

1799-1800
The British Parliament passes the Combination Acts, forbidding the formation of groups for the purpose of political reform and making it illegal to interfere with trade. The laws were used to ban trades unions.

1802
The British Parliament passes the first Factory Act, regulating conditions for child workers in cotton and woollen mills – and limiting their work to 12 hours a day. However, it makes no provision for inspections, and is to be widely ignored.

1804
Corn laws are introduced to protect landed establishment farmers from cheaper food imports – tariffs keep the price of bread at artificially high levels.

1807
Parliament prohibits owning or importing slaves in the UK. Slavery in British colonies is abolished in 1834.

1811-1813
Machine-breaking disturbances rock the wool and cotton industries, becoming known as the 'Luddite riots'. These begin in Nottingham in 1811 and are named after the mythical 'General Ned Ludd', who supposedly led the movement from Sherwood Forest. Later, Yorkshire and Lancashire become the hubs of dissent – the protests focus on the introduction of power looms and low wages. Machine-breaking is made punishable by death in 1812, and some 20 people are executed shortly thereafter.

1813
Robert Owen publishes *A New View of Society*, outlining his reforms at New Lanark and encouraging the development of self-supporting 'villages of co-operation' as a means of improving living and working conditions and creating 'a new moral world'.

1819
The Peterloo Massacre: 15 are killed and between 400-700 injured in Manchester, England, as the Yeomanry charges a crowd demonstrating for Parliamentary reform.

1824
The Combination Acts in the UK are repealed but laws passed in 1825 narrowly define trade union rights and place severe limits on the right to strike.

1828
Dr William King publishes *The Co-operator*, one of the most significant journals of the time. When it ended its monthly publication in 1830, *The Co-operator* reported that there were at least 300 co-operatives in Britain.

1830
Charles Lyell's *Principles of Geology* is published, disproving the creationist view of the Earth being a mere 6,000 years old. It influences the thinking of the young Charles Darwin.

Peterloo Massacre, 1819.

1830s
British rural communities protest against the loss of traditional livelihoods and onset of mechanization, destroying agricultural machinery in the name of the fictional Captain Swing.

1831
Owen organizes the first Co-operative Congress, in Manchester. Altogether eight such congresses are held between 1831 and 1835.

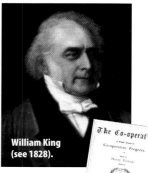
William King (see 1828).

1832
The First Reform Act in Britain ends 'rotten boroughs', and narrowly expands voting rights. Around one in seven adult men have the vote, but most working-class men and all women are excluded.

1833-1847
Britain's Parliament passes a series of three further Factory Acts (1833, 1844 & 1847) that progressively restrict the time women and children are allowed to work. The 1833 Act specifies that no child under the age of nine should work. The 1847 Act states that women and children under 18 years of age should not work more than ten hours a day. The

basic notion that males over the age of 18 should work a 15-hour day from, say, 5.30am to 8.30pm remains unchallenged. This leads to the typical working man being stunted in growth and subject to a range of debilitating illnesses.

1834
Six workers in Dorset, England, are charged with swearing an illegal oath when they meet to form a trade union, protesting their low wages. The 'Tolpuddle Martyrs' are sentenced to seven years' transportation to a penal colony in Australia. More than 800,000 sign a petition to Parliament protesting the sentences, which are eventually commuted.

1836
Charles Darwin formulates his thoughts on the transmutation of species while journeying on *HMS Beagle* but delays wide publication fearing the reaction of the church and wider scientific establishment. He is eventually spurred to publication by the discovery in 1848 that Alfred Russel Wallace is advancing his own theories of evolution via natural selection.

1837-1844
In the period known as the Hungry Forties, more than a million paupers starve in the worst economic depression ever to afflict the British people. East Lancashire and West Yorkshire are hotbeds of discontent. As early as 1795, there had been 'food riots' in Rochdale, when two men were killed. In 1808, a dispute in Rochdale between handloom weavers and their employers, some of whom were failing to keep to the agreed wage standard, led to the 'shuttle gathering'

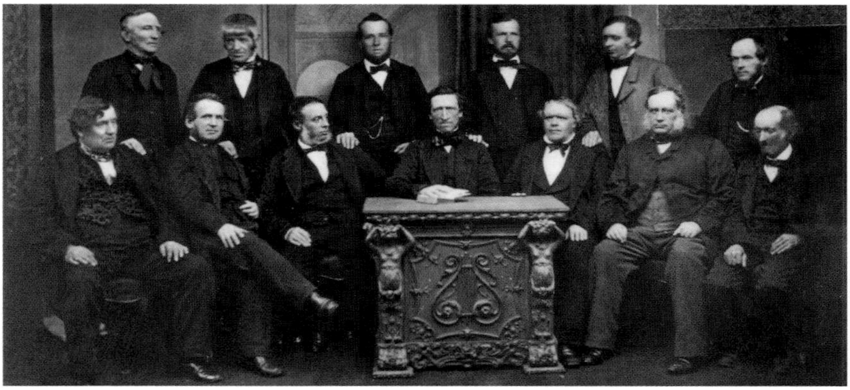

Thirteen of the original Rochdale Pioneers, pictured at the dawn of photography in the 1860s.

riots. This resulted in a militia marching into the town to quell the riot; it was to remain for many years.

1838
The People's Charter is published in Britain, establishing the Chartist movement and six key demands, including universal male suffrage. Although seen as radical at the time, five of these 'six points' are adopted by 1918.

Parliament refuses to consider a Chartist petition of 1.2 million. As a result there are riots in Birmingham and Newport. Chartist leaders are imprisoned.

Charles Dickens' second novel, *Oliver Twist*, is published. It shines a light on the atrocious treatment of children by Victorian society, not least in workhouses.

1839
Manchester entrepreneur Richard Cobden unites separate anti-corn law associations into a single Anti-Corn Law League. Lancashire-born, reforming Conservative prime minister, Robert Peel, is to lead the repeal of corn laws in 1846 – and then be promptly removed from office by landed MPs.

1842
A third of the British population petitions Parliament in support of Chartism – to little effect.

1843
Charles Dickens visits Manchester and witnesses child poverty in excess of that which he has seen in London. He sets to writing a new novel that will 'strike a hammer blow for the poor man's child' – *A Christmas Carol*.

1844
Friedrich Engels publishes *The Condition of the English Working Class*, describing squalid conditions in Manchester, the first city in the world to industrialize.

The Rochdale Society of Equitable Pioneers opens on 21 December, creating a successful co-operative model that becomes the blueprint for UK consumer co-operatives and goes on to inspire today's global movement.

1846
Eliza Brierley becomes the first recorded female member of the Rochdale Pioneers Society, which allowed men and women to be members with equal rights and responsibilities, including voting rights.

1848
Beginning in France, a series of unco-ordinated revolutions topple existing governments and seek more democratic participation. Many European countries experience serious revolts, including Germany, Italy and Austria. Karl Marx and Friedrich Engels publish *The Communist Manifesto*.

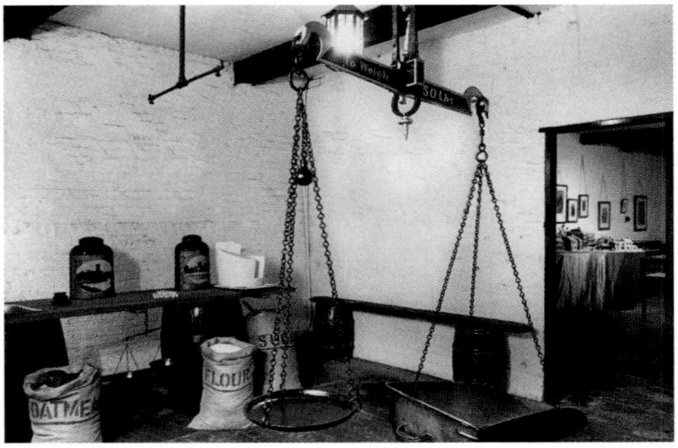
FLOUR

A recreation of the Rochdale Pioneers' first store.

Christian Socialists form in London, and promote co-operatives as a peaceful alternative to the revolutions occurring in Europe.

The third Chartist petition is presented in London. Fear of revolution leads to special constables being recruited in all major cities. Lack of progress sees Chartism in its purest form wane.

1849
The Rochdale Pioneers open their first reading room and elect an education committee. The Pioneers devoted 2.5 per cent of the society's profits to fund reading rooms, libraries, lectures, and classes for members and their children.

Alfred, Lord Tennyson's poem 'In Memoriam A.H.H.' introduces the phrase 'Nature, red in tooth and claw'.

1852
Germany's Herman Schulze-Delitzsch founds a 'people's bank' to provide credit to entrepreneurs in his home city – now recognized as the world's first credit union.

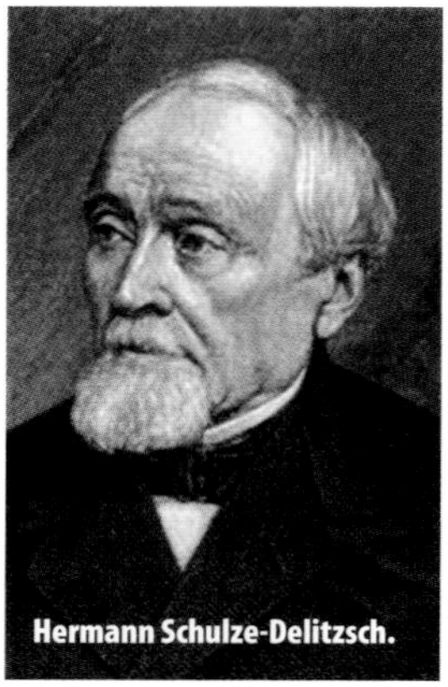
Hermann Schulze-Delitzsch.
portrait.kaar.at

Parliament passes the Industrial and Provident Societies Act (drafted by Christian Socialist EV Neale), providing the first legal framework for co-operatives; a revision in 1862 allows for co-operative federations.

1857
George Jacob Holyoake publishes the first history of the Rochdale Pioneers, helping to spread the Rochdale model of consumer co-operation. It is eventually published in several European languages and runs to multiple editions.

1859
Charles Darwin publishes *On the Origin of Species by Means of Natural Selection* and creates a firestorm of controversy for his implied claim that humans have evolved from other animals. Only later, in 1871, does he deal in detail with the human elements of his work, in *The Descent of Man, and Selection in Relation to Sex.*

The first known consumer co-operative in Australia is founded in Brisbane.

1860
The Manchester Equitable Co-operative Society begins publishing *The Co-operator,* a national monthly journal edited by Henry Pitman (brother of shorthand's inventor). Though it takes the same name as William King's journal, this is a new publication. It advocates setting up a co-operative wholesale agency.

In Italy, credit co-operative societies are organized by Luigi Luzzatti; consumer co-operatives soon follow, forming a League of Co-operative Societies.

1861
The US Civil War begins, ending in 1865. The blockade of the Confederate states causes a 'cotton famine' in UK manufacturing districts, leading to widespread unemployment. Yet co-operators, workers and the UK government continue to back the Northern states' stance against slavery.

1863
The North of England Co-operative Wholesale Society (CWS) is established. It is a 'co-operative of co-operatives' in which local societies become members. The new organization is necessary because private wholesalers often refuse to supply co-operatives or charge high prices. The new CWS adopts the motto 'Labor and Wait', spelling it so in solidarity with the US battle against slavery.

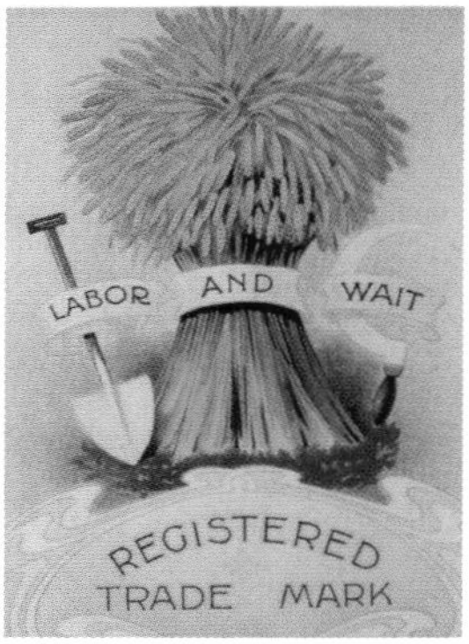
LABOR AND WAIT
REGISTERED
TRADE MARK

The Rochdale model of co-operation spreads quickly around the country. Within 20 years, more than 350 other co-operative societies have sprung up, which between them have a membership of over 100,000.

1864
Germany's Frederick Wilhelm Raiffessen establishes his first rural credit co-operative society. Together with Schulze-Delitzsch, these form the basis for modern credit unions. A central credit union was established in 1869.

1867
The UK Parliament passes the Second Reform Act, doubling the number of adult men eligible to vote.

The Co-operative Insurance is established to help cover co-ops in case of fires or other damage to their premises, as private insurers often refused to deal with co-operatives.

The Grange is established in Washington DC to promote mutual and co-operative organization among US farmers. Today, it is the oldest surviving agricultural organization in the US.

1868
The Trades Union Congress (TUC) holds its first Congress, in Manchester, England; a separate Scottish TUC is formed in 1897.

The Scottish Co-operative Wholesale Society is set up on similar lines to the CWS.

1869
The first of the modern series of Co-operative Congresses is held in London; it is still an annual event today.

1870
The UK Parliament passes the Education Act, setting up the first state system of primary education in England and Wales and requiring schooling for children up to the age of ten. The first Married Women's Property Act is also passed, for the first time giving wives the right to own property in their own names.

Following the first Co-operative Congress, societies form the Co-operative Union, a national body providing information, educational resources and legal advice to co-operatives as well as informing the wider public. This body is today known as Co-operative UK.

1871
The Co-operative News begins publication, providing the growing movement with its first weekly newspaper. It has been in continuous publication ever since.

1872
CWS drops 'North of England' from its name (reflecting its growth to include all of England and Wales) and forms a Loan and Deposit Department (the precursor of today's Co-operative Bank) to meet the financial needs of co-operative societies.

1873
CWS opens its first factories to produce co-operative branded goods, in Manchester (biscuits) and Leicester (boots).

1874
CWS sets up a London branch and opens a purchasing depot in New York (its first outside the British Isles).

1875
In the US, the Grange approves Rochdale principles as the basis for establishing a network of co-operative stores, grain elevators, banks, and insurance companies.

1878
Membership of UK consumer co-operatives tops 500,000.

1881
SCWS opens its first factory, in Glasgow (making shirts).

1882
In the US, Harvard students organize a co-operative bookstore: 'the Coop', which is still operating today.

The Co-operative Productive Federation is organized to promote worker co-operation in the UK.

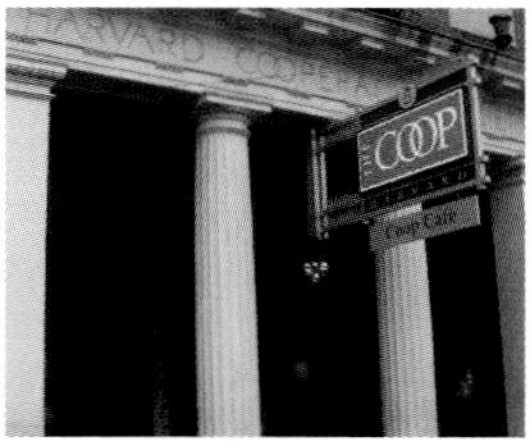
COOP
Elena Vilalta

Harvard Coop store (see 1882).

1883
The Co-operative Women's Guild is established, seeking to improve the position of women in co-operatives and in society generally.

1884
The UK's Third Reform Act triples the number of men eligible to vote to about 60 per cent of adult males.

1887
The first Co-operative Act in Canada is passed by the Manitoba legislature.

1890
The first women (six) are elected to co-operative management committees in England & Wales. The Co-operative Women's Guild encourages members to stand for co-operative positions and local government offices where women are eligible, including as Poor Law Guardians.

The Swiss co-operative wholesale society, VSK, is established.

1891
Membership of UK consumer co-ops tops one million.

1893
German biologist Andreas Schimper speculates that the photosynthetic parts of plant cells come from bacteria.

The Independent Labour Party is founded in Bradford. Yorkshire and Lancashire contingents dominate the party in its early years.

1894
The Manchester Ship Canal opens – then the largest river navigation canal in the world. In recognition of the significant financial investment made by the CWS and other co-operatives, the SS Pioneer (a CWS steamship) is the first to travel the length of the canal.

In Germany, consumer societies found a co-operative wholesale society, GEG.

1895
The International Co-operative Alliance (ICA) is founded in London, to connect co-operative movements in different countries. The Congress includes representatives from nine European countries, Argentina, Australia, India and the US.

California passes the first US state co-operative law, introducing one-member, one-vote; other states begin to adopt similar laws.

1896
The CWS purchases its first farm in Roden, Shropshire. Today The Co-operative is one of Britain's largest farmers.

1897
The UK campaign for women's suffrage gains momentum with the formation of the National Union of Women's Suffrage Societies.

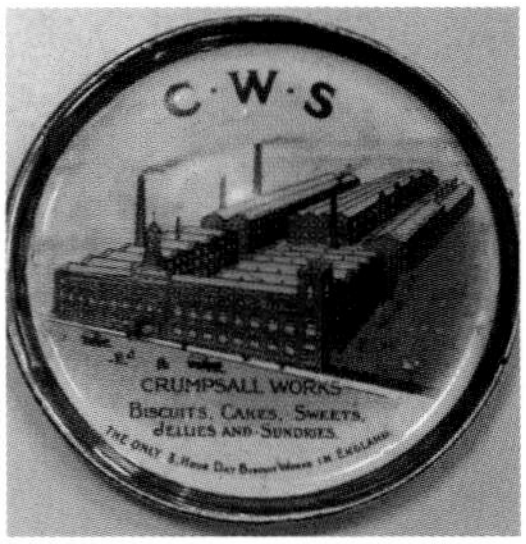
C·W·S
CRUMPSALL WORKS
BISCUITS, CAKES, SWEETS, JELLIES AND SUNDRIES

A coaster acknowledging CWS Crumpsall as the only biscuit factory in England with an eight-hour working day.

1898
Centrosoyuz, the central union of consumer co-operatives, is founded in Russia.

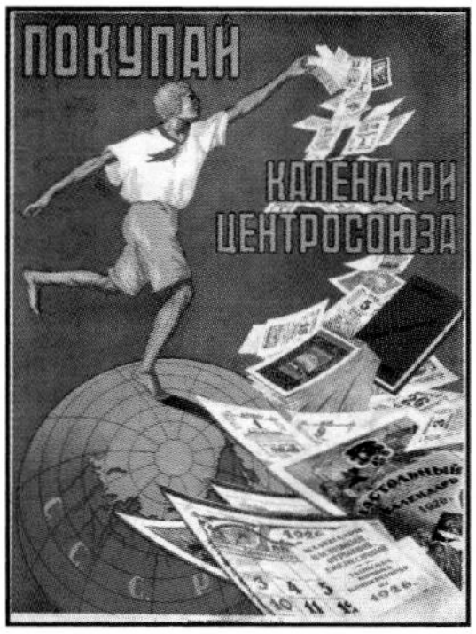
ПОКУПАЙ
КАЛЕНДАРИ
ЦЕНТРОСОЮЗА
kitchener.lord

1899
In Sweden, Kooperative Forbundet (KF) is founded; within ten years it is both the central co-operative union and the co-operative wholesale society.

1900
Quebec's Levis Credit Union, the first to be established in North America, is founded by Alphonse Desjardins; by 1909 there are more than 100 credit unions in Quebec.

Japan passes a law covering consumer, marketing and utility co-operatives, as well as credit societies.

1902
CWS and SCWS jointly purchase estates in Ceylon (now Sri Lanka) as a source of tea; they later purchase similar estates in India.

1904
The membership of UK consumer co-operatives tops two million.

CWS employees form a Thrift Fund as a provision against old age; in 1907 this becomes a pension scheme, with CWS supplementing employee contributions.

India passes a Co-operative Credit Societies Act, allowing for Raiffeisen-style agricultural credit societies; the law influenced other co-operative legislation throughout the British empire.

1906
Leading co-operator George Holyoake dies.

The Proprietary Articles Traders Association (PATA) refuses to supply patent medicines to co-operatives paying dividend on these. CWS closes accounts with PATA members and extends its own drug manufacturing.

In Finland, co-operative wholesaling and education are combined in one national organization, NKL.

1909
The first US credit union is established, in Manchester, New Hampshire; the Co-operative Union of Canada is established; and the Czech Co-operative Wholesale Society is formed.

1912
The Federation of Consumer Co-operatives is founded in France.

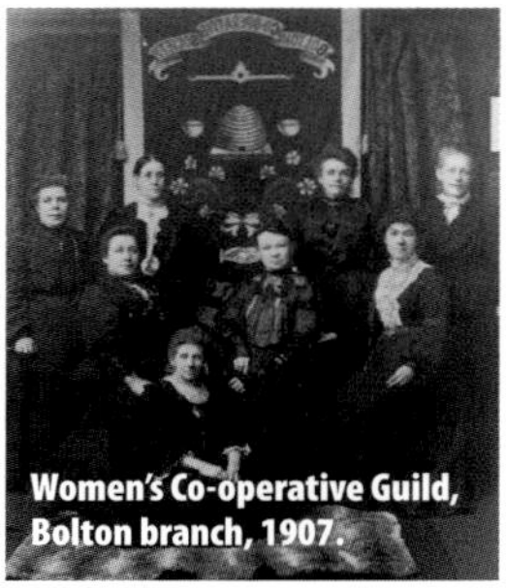
Women's Co-operative Guild, Bolton branch, 1907.

1913
CWS and SCWS jointly purchase the Co-operative Insurance Society and set up the first African Depot in Gold Coast (now Ghana).

In the US, President Taft establishes a commission to study European co-ops and credit societies.

The Co-operative Women's Guild leads a successful campaign for National Insurance maternity benefits to be paid directly to mothers.

1914
The First World War begins on 4 August.

Co-operative societies, including the Wholesales, begin running army canteens. The CWS obtains government contracts for military clothing and other necessary items. During the War, many co-operative factories are converted to war work or requisitioned by the British government.

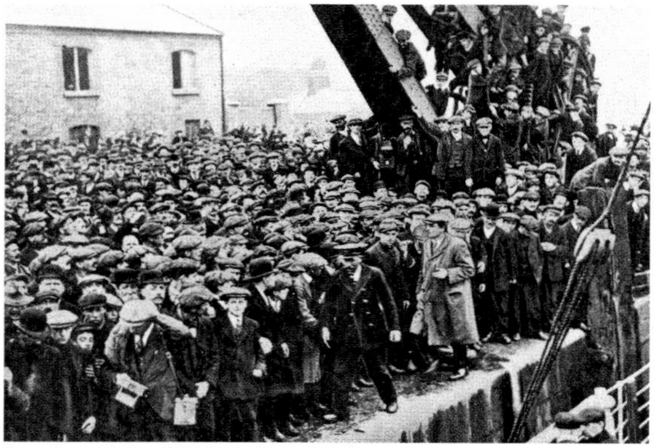
Crowds awaiting CWS food ships , Dublin, 1913.

Membership of UK consumer co-operatives tops three million.

In the US, the first electric non-profit co-operatives, forerunners of rural electric co-operatives, are founded.

1916
During the First World War some UK co-operative societies begin to issue 'sugar cards' to ration scarce commodities and ensure fair distribution to members. Many societies take up voluntary rationing and expand their programmes to other scarce items, until government rationing begins in 1918.

In the US, the Cooperative League of America is founded, the forerunner of today's National Cooperative Business Association.

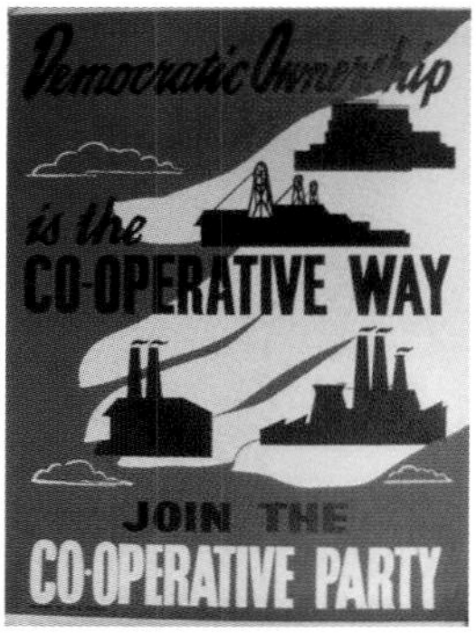
Democratic Ownership
is the
CO-OPERATIVE WAY
JOIN THE
CO-OPERATIVE PARTY

1917
The Co-operative Party is established, following widespread dissatisfaction with the lack of co-operative appointments to government food control committees and military tribunals, inadequate supplies to co-operative stores, and the imposition of Excess Profits Duty on members' dividends in 1915.

1918
In Britain, the Representation of the People Act is passed; it grants voting rights to all men over 21 and women over 30.

The League of Nations is formed – the first permanent intergovernmental organization aimed at preventing conflict.

The ICA presses for recognition by the League of Nations, but does not receive even limited advisory recognition until 1922.

The International Labour Organization, which includes a co-operative branch, is created by the Treaty of Versailles.

The Co-operative College is established in Manchester, providing research, education and training for co-operative employees and members.

Membership of UK consumer co-operatives tops four million.

1921
The International Co-operative Women's Guild is formed.

Mary Cottrell becomes the first woman elected to the Board of CWS, then one of Britain's largest businesses.

1923
The ICA establishes the first International Co-operative Day, which is still celebrated by co-operative members around the world on the first Saturday in July.

1926
Membership of UK consumer co-operatives tops five million.

1928
Britain's Equal Franchise Act grants voting rights to all men and women over 21.

The National Federation of Co-operatives in Spain is established.

"DEFIANT" RADIO RECEIVERS
Pleasing to the ear
TWELVE NEW SEASONS MODELS ALL GIVING EXCELLENT RESULTS

1929
Membership of UK consumer co-operatives tops six million.

1933
Retail radio dealers ask CWS not to apply a dividend to radio sets or face a boycott. The CWS rejects the proposal and begins to manufacture radios, selling them under the name Defiant.

1934
Membership of UK consumer co-operatives tops seven million.
Both CWS and SCWS open Funeral Departments, assisting societies in providing funeralcare.

1936
A group of 200 unemployed workers from Jarrow (near Newcastle) march to London, seeking government aid for the hard-hit town.

Throughout the Jarrow March, many co-operative societies offer food and shelter. When the march reaches Leicester, co-operative workers labour overnight to repair their boots, turning out 112 mended pairs.

US President Franklin D Roosevelt sends another commission to study the role of co-operatives in Europe.

1937
Membership of UK consumer co-ops tops eight million.

1938
Britain's Holidays With Pay Act recommends, but does not mandate, one week's annual paid holiday to all full-time workers.

In Mexico, the first general law for co-operative societies is passed; a Mexican Co-operative League for consumer and workers co-ops had already been established.

1939
The Second World War begins, on 3 September.

By the start of the War, fascist governments had destroyed or taken over established co-operative movements in Austria, Czechoslovakia, Germany, Italy and Spain. On Adolf Hitler's birthday Nazis present him with a million deutschmarks stolen from co-operative funds.

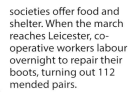

The Co-operative Congress in the shadow of war, Margete, 1939.

In the UK, many co-operative factories are converted once again to war work or requisitioned by government (for instance, the SCWS sheet metal works at Shieldhall produces the top-secret 'flying dustbin' shells used for the Normandy landings). Co-operative leaders are included on most wartime committees related to industry and food control from the start of the conflict.

1940
The number of people registered with co-operatives for rationed goods tops 13.5 million – around 23 per cent of the UK population.

1942
The London Co-operative Society introduces the first self-service shopping in the UK, converting part of its Romford branch as part of a wartime experiment. Five years later, the Portsea Island Co-operative Society becomes the first fully self-service store in the UK.

In the US, the National Rural Electric Cooperative Association is formed.
Co-operative stores are organized by Japanese-Americans in internment camps.

1945
The Second World War ends in Europe, on 7 May.

The United Nations is established, replacing the League of Nations.

The ICA becomes one of the first international non-governmental organizations to receive UN consultative status. The Alliance leads a fundraising effort to help rebuild co-operative movements in Austria, Italy and Germany,

The CO-OP flag covers the world

and other countries where co-operatives had been effectively abolished.

The Cooperative for American Remittances to Europe (CARE) is formed to provide food and other assistance to war-ravaged Europe – the food aid they send is the origin of the term 'care package'; CARE is later to provide aid to areas outside Europe.

1948
Credit Union Day is established, to celebrate the 100th anniversary of credit unions in Germany.

1953
Co-operatives account for around 66 per cent of all self-service shops in Britain – around 2.5 times the amount run by large multiple food stores.

1954
The US national association for credit unions develops its World Extension Division, set up to spread credit union ideas globally, particularly in developing countries.

1955
CWS is among the first businesses to advertise its products on the new Independent Television Network (ITN), with a campaign called 'Spot the Likeness' mirroring popular quiz shows of the time.

1956
Mondragon, the world's largest worker co-operative, is founded in Spain in response to General Franco's dictatorship.

1958
The Co-operative Independent Commission, established in 1955, highlights challenges for the co-operative movement in facing increased retail competition. Its report lays the groundwork for a series of reforms in the movement, including many mergers of independent co-operative societies.

1960
The first ICA regional office opens in India, to assist growing co-operative movements in the Asia-Pacific region.

1965
Co-operative societies launch dividend stamps in response to the adoption of trading stamps by other food retailers. CWS launches a national scheme in 1969.

1967
In Santos, Brazil, the healthcare co-operative Unimed is founded; it now operates throughout the country and represents nearly a third of all doctors practising in Brazil.

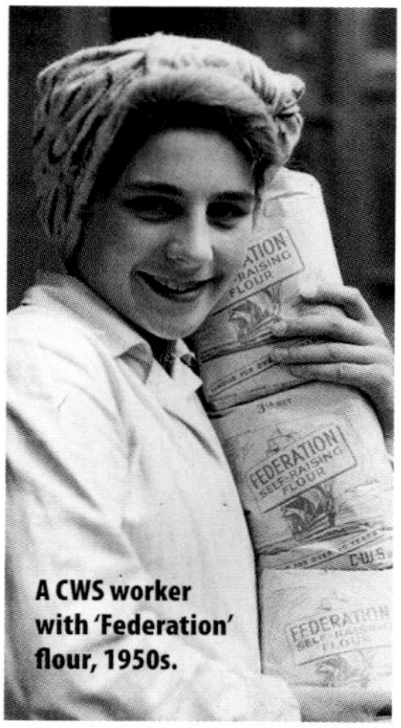
FEDERATION
SELF-RAISING
FLOUR
A CWS worker with 'Federation' flour, 1950s.

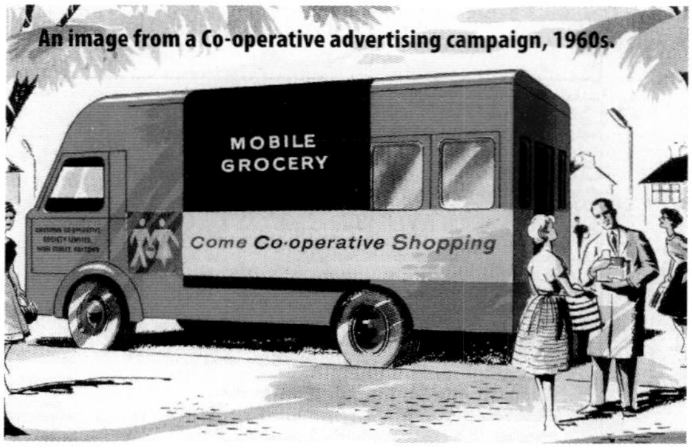
MOBILE
GROCERY
Come Co-operative Shopping
An image from a Co-operative advertising campaign, 1960s.

Unimed
Brasil

1968
The ICA Regional Office for East, Central and South Africa opens, to support growing co-operative movements in Africa; a separate West African office is opened in 1975.

CWS launches its first national advertising campaign using the new 'Co-op' logo, as part of a widespread campaign to modernize co-operative shops and branding.

1969
In the UK, the voting age is lowered to 18.

1970
The World Council of Credit Unions is formed.

Lynn Margulis publishes a book arguing that animal and plant cells evolved via a series of endosymbiotic steps. Initially ridiculed, this is now textbook orthodoxy.

1973
CWS and SCWS merge, creating Britain's 10th-largest business at the time.

1974
The Co-operative Bank becomes the first in the UK to offer free current accounts to personal banking customers.

1976
The Industrial Common Ownership Act is passed, granting seed funding to the Industrial Common Ownership Movement (ICOM), which is to support the creation of over 2,000 worker co-ops by the end of the century.

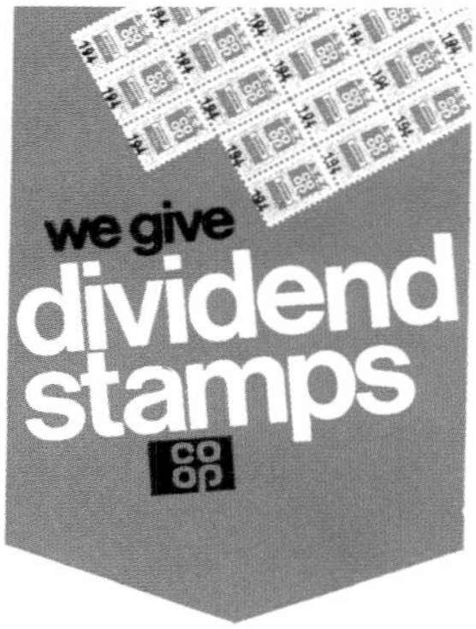
we give
dividend
stamps
co
op
Launch of dividend stamps (see 1965).

Richard Dawkins' *The Selfish Gene* is published, amidst an established scientific push to (successfully) relegate the idea of 'group selection' to the levels of absurdity.

1978
The Co-operative Development Agency (CDA) is set up by the government to promote co-operative initiatives.

1979
Families in Denmark work together to install a 55kW wind turbine. Within 20 years, co-operatives like theirs make Denmark a world leader in renewable energy.

1989
Abbey National becomes the UK's first building society to demutualize, converting to a private bank; over the next decade many other building societies follow suit.

The second edition of Richard Dawkins' *The Selfish Gene* is published. At a time when its central message has become textbook orthodoxy, a new chapter is introduced entitled 'Nice Guys Finish First', which describes how co-operation can evolve.

1990
The ICA regional office for the Americas is established in San José, Costa Rica, to support co-operative movements in the Western Hemishpere.

1992
The Co-operative Bank launches its groundbreakig Ethical Policy.

The Co-operative becomes the first major UK retailer to champion fairly traded products. It goes on to become the first to stock Fairtrade bananas in the UK (2000) and the first to convert all its own-brand hot beverages to Fairtrade (2008).

1994
CWS sells its food manufacturing operations, focusing instead on wholesale supply, food retailing, and operations in specialist retail areas such as travel, pharmacy, and funeralcare.

1995
The Co-operative Values & Principles statement

is launched at the ICA centennial meeting in Manchester. It remains the key document in global terms defining what it means to be a co-operative.

The Co-operative becomes the first UK supermarket to ban animal testing of its own-brand toiletries.

1997
CWS successfully averts an attempt at a hostile takeover that sought to demutualize CWS and sell its assets; the following year, members vote to strengthen rules to prevent future takeover attempts.

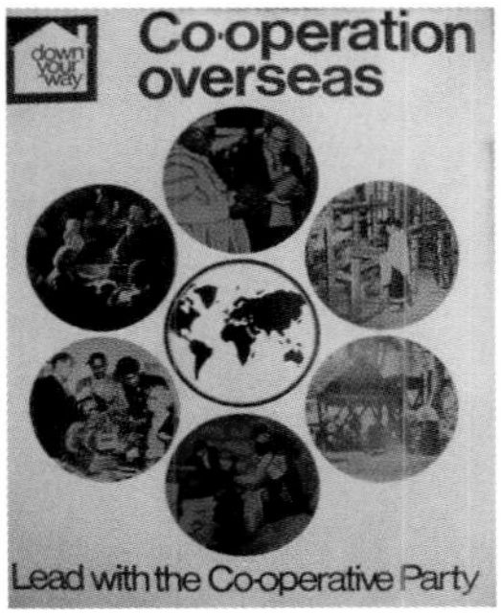
Co-operation overseas
down your way
Lead with the Co-operative Party

1998
The Co-operative Bank produces its first 'warts and all' Sustainability Report. The high standard of reporting leads to numerous awards from across the world in subsequent years.

1999
CWS becomes the first retailer to stock Fairtrade products in every food store.

The Co-operative Bank launches smile, the UK's first full internet bank.

2000
CWS and CRS merge to form The Co-operative Group.

2002
The Co-operative Group becomes the first retailer to transition all own-brand block chocolate to Fairtrade; the following year it does the same with all own-brand coffee.

The Co-operative Union and the Industrial Common Ownership Movement merge to form Co-operatives UK.

2006
The Co-operative Group reintroduces the dividend across the UK and begins an extensive rebranding programme across its entire 'family of businesses'.

David Sloan Wilson and Edward O Wilson submit a paper to *Science* arguing that biological systems are a nested hierarchy of units, from genes within individuals, individuals within groups, groups within a population and even clusters of groups. This originates Multi-level Selection Theory.

The third edition of Richard Dawkins' *The Selfish Gene* is published. In a new introduction the author admits to having second thoughts on the title of the book. He speculates that 'The Immortal Gene', 'The Altruistic Vehicle' and perhaps even 'The Co-operative Gene' might have been better titles (given that self-interested genes can co-operate).

2007
United Co-operatives (which had the Rochdale Pioneers as a direct predecessor) merges with The Co-operative Group to create a national retail co-operative for the first time. Chief Executive, Peter Marks, announces that the business needs rapid growth in scale if it is to compete effectively.

2008
The collapse of the US housing market and international banks' involvement leads to global financial crisis. The UK government responds by taking failing banks into public ownership. At the peak of the crisis, nationalized banks owe the UK government more than £1 trillion ($1.6 trillion).

The Co-operative Bank needs no government assistance during the crisis and sees its banking business and customer satisfaction levels increase.

The Co-operative Group purchases Somerfield's supermarket chain, doubling its share of the retail food market to become the UK's fifth-largest food retailer.

Reddish Vale Technology College becomes the first Co-operative Trust School in the UK – there are now more than 240.

2009
The Co-operative Bank and Britannia Building Society merge.

The Co-operative Enterprise Hub is established to advise and assist new co-operatives and further build the UK's co-operative economy.

Elinor Ostrom is awarded the Nobel Prize for Economic Science for demonstrating how people frequently manage common resources co-operatively.

2010
The Co-operative Bank is recognized as Europe's most sustainable bank by the *Financial Times*. It receives the same accolade in 2011 and 2012.

2011
Rochdale is declared to be the world capital of co-operatives by the

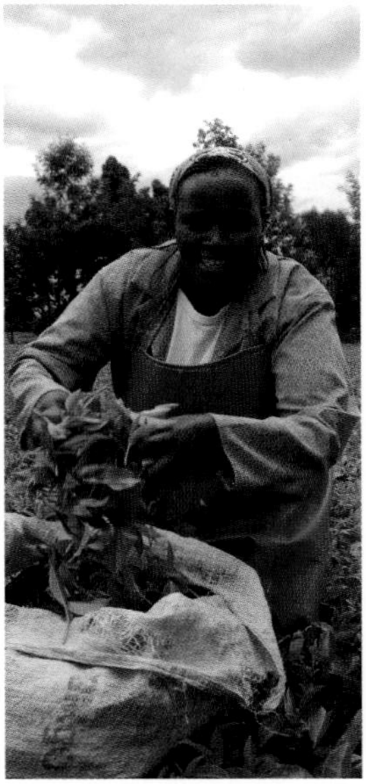

Picking tea in Kenya for The Co-operative's Fairtrade 99 Tea.

general assembly of the International Co-operative Alliance.

The Co-operative launches its Ethical Plan – the most radical sustainability programme in UK corporate history, demonstrating that the quiet revolution that began in Rochdale in 1844 is as relevant as ever.

2012
The UN declares this the International Year of Co-operatives.

Over 13 million people in the UK are now members of a co-operative.

Globally , there are now 1.4 million co-operatives, which between them have nearly one billion members and provide over 100 million jobs.

All images used by permission of the National Co-operative Archive, Manchester, UK, unless otherwise indicated.

2012 International Year of Co-operatives

Take action:

Send a message to the UK Government to help Grow Co-operatives.

www.co-operative.coop/grow

Betty Chesang is among 11,000 Kenyan smallholder tea producers in the Kericho region who have formed five co-operatives. Globally, there are 500 million smallholder farmers who together feed nearly a third of humanity. We believe with the right tools, training and investment, these smallholder farmers – many of whom are women – offer an excellent route to help sustainably feed the world's growing population. What's more, if supported to form co-operatives, this enables them to pool resources, increase yields and secure fairer prices.

Alongside Oxfam, we're calling on the UK Government to unlock greater support for smallholder farmers and co-operatives to feed the world fairly and sustainably.